THE DALAI LAMA

About Wyatt North Publishing

Starting out with just one writer, Wyatt North Publishing has expanded to include writers from across the country. Our writers include college professors, religious theologians, and historians.

Wyatt North Publishing provides high quality, perfectly formatted, original books.

Send us an email and we will personally respond within 24 hours! As a boutique publishing company we put our readers first and never respond with canned or automated emails. Send us an email at hello@WyattNorth.com, and you can visit us at www.WyattNorth.com.

Introduction

Nothing about the birth of Lhamo Dhondup marked him for greatness. He arrived the way all children do in the village of Taktser, a farming community in the mountains of Tibet. In 1935, the year of Lhamo Dhondup's birth, Taktser featured thirty or so dwellings, cobbled together from stone and mud. Dhondup was the fifth child born to a family that would eventually have seven children who survived the perils of infancy and several others who did not.

To the casual observer, nothing marked the baby Lhamo Dhondup as someone who would one day winter in a palace with a thousand rooms and travel under escort of colorfully costumed cavalry, high-ranking army officers, porters, musicians, troops of monks, and pet songbirds.

In Amdo, the province to which Taktser belonged, poverty was so entrenched that it was customary for at least one child of any family—usually a son—to be sent to a monastery in order to relieve the family of the expense of feeding and clothing him. Deprivation was so dire that, according to Lhamo Dhondup's mother, a young couple once showed up on her doorstep with a dead child. Upon offering to help them give the child a proper burial, she learned that they intended to eat the child instead.

Lhamo Dhondup's family, by contrast, was reasonably financially stable. They were subsistence farmers who produced little surplus but whose hard-earned crops consistently put food on the family's table. They grew barley, potatoes, and buckwheat. Irrigation systems were unheard of, and their crops were at the mercy of rain and drought. They raised livestock, including chickens, sheep, goats, and dzomos—a domestic breed of cattle derived from crossing cows and yaks. They also kept horses and purebred yaks. Lhamo Dhondup's father occasionally traded a sheep or some grain for tea, sugar, cloth, ornaments, or utensils.

Meals at Lhamo Dhondup's house were simple affairs, almost always featuring tsampa, a flour derived from roasted barley and mixed with tea, milk, yoghurt, or beer. The taste for tsampa is generally acquired at a young age or not at all.

They were a conventional family living in a conventional house, almost entirely like those of their neighbors but with one exception. Lhamo Dhondup's house featured rain gutters, which were made of crudely carved juniper. This minor variation in architectural taste would play a huge role in the future of Lhamo Dhondup and the country of Tibet. By this and other small architectural tokens, the future spiritual and temporal leader of the Tibetan Buddhists would be identified.

As a child, Lhamo Dhondup already demonstrated some of the telling qualities of a spiritual leader. Once, upon observing children playing a war game, he rushed to assist the weaker side. He abhorred quarrels but insisted on a place at the head of the table. And one of his favorite games was packing his suitcase. It was as if he knew he was destined for leadership and world travel.

Two years prior to Lhamo Dhondup's birth, his former incarnation—the thirteenth Dalai Lama—died suddenly of a virus. After his death, the monks surrounding him immediately began looking for signs that would lead them to his next incarnation. Buddhists believe that, at the highest level of spiritual achievement, a holy man may choose the circumstances of his next life. So, after the death of the thirteenth Lama, it was the job of Buddhist leaders to discover where he had chosen to be reborn.

Several signs told the Buddhist leaders that the next Dalai Lama would be born in Tibet's northeast. The deceased Dalai Lama had been laid to rest with his head pointing south and, for no logical reason that the leaders could discover, his head moved so that he was facing the northeast. Meanwhile a star-shaped accumulation of moss grew on the northeast pillar of his tomb, and storms brewed over the skies of that part of the country.

The Buddhist leaders elected a regent to discover the identity of the fourteenth Lama. That regent went to a holy lake and had a vision of the house that the newly incarnate Dalai Lama was born in. In the regent's vision, the fourteenth Dalai Lama was living in a house with distinctive guttering near a monastery with a roof of turquoise tile.

The leaders sent a search party to quest for the fourteenth Dalai Lama. This party discovered that the Kumbum monastery in Amdo was roofed with turquoise tiles. Nearby was a house with strange gutters, just as indicated in the regent's vision.

The search party's leader, Kewtsang Rinpoche, paid an initial visit to the house where the Dalai Lama was suspected to have been reborn. He did not, however, reveal the nature of his business until he had made a reconnaissance. He approached the family pretending to be a humble servant, but young

Lhamo Dhondup, not yet three years old, outed him instantly, calling him "Sera Lama." "Lama" identified the man as a monk, and Sera was the name of the monastery to which he belonged.

A few days later, the search party returned to administer a test. They brought a number of toys, some of which had belonged to the departed Dalai Lama and others of which had no relevance. They presented the toys to Lhamo Dhondup, who correctly identified all of those that had belonged to the prior Lama and noted, "They're mine!"

Lhamo Dhondup, from the humble village of Taktser, was thereby found to be the fourteenth incarnation of the Dalai Lama, the spiritual leader of Tibetan Gelug Buddhism, which had been founded in the 1300s.

A few months later, Lhamo Dhondup's new role forced him to leave his family and live in the Kumbum monastery. By his own report, he was miserable at being separated from his parents, and his only real consolation during his time in Kumbum was the companionship of his brother, Lobsang Samden. Lobsang Samden was three years older than Lhamo

Dhondup, and he was already living at the monastery when the toddler Dalai Lama arrived.

Both boys were eventually reunited with their family for the trip to Lhasa, where the new Dalai Lama would be formally inducted into his role. The journey took three months, as the travelers had to cross a high mountain range in a mule-drawn palanquin. A huge encampment had been constructed outside the capital to welcome the boy. It was there, in a ceremony that took an entire day, that Lhamo Dhondup was officially recognized as the Dalai Lama. Another ceremony marked the boy's arrival at the winter palace of Potala, where he was first seated on a bedazzled lion throne.

Yet another ceremony marked the new Lama's arrival at Jokhang Temple, where he would be formally trained as a monk. Where the earlier ceremonies had involved pomp and circumstance, hinting of a wealthy and powerful future, the ceremony of induction to the Jokhang Temple involved symbolic gestures of humility and self-denial. The five-year old's head was shaved, and he was dressed in a relatively simple wine-colored robe. He relinquished the name his parents gave him and became instead Jamphel Ngawang Lobsang Yeshe Tensiz Gyatso, or Jamphel Yeshe for short.

The Calm Before the Storm

From the ages of six to eight, Jamphel Yeshe received private lessons alongside his brother Lobsang Samden. Their upbringing was a study in contradictions. As monks, they were taught the virtue of self denial—to dress simply, keep their heads shaved, avoid eating meat, and abstain from sex. Whips were kept in plain site during lessons with the threat that, if the child were lazy and failed to learn, he would feel the whip's bite.

At the same time, Jamphel Yeshe moved every year between a summer home and a winter home—a luxury unheard of for most Tibetans. In the winters, he was installed in the equivalent of a penthouse suite at the top of the seven-story Potala Palace. His every need and whim were fulfilled by one servant or another. He and his brother had three dedicated tutors and a small staff of "masters." One monk was assigned to be Jamphel Yeshe's master of robes, another his master of the kitchen, and yet another his master of rituals. The young Dalai Lama did not even have to clean or sweep his own room. A fleet of attendants were assigned to that chore, but they were never too busy to stop and play with the Lama should he require a companion. While other monks in training were routinely whipped with whips made of leather straps, the whip reserved for the Dalai Lama was made of yellow silk. It was not once deployed. The closest the monks came to whipping Jamphel Yeshe was to whip his brother in his sight. With his characteristic wisdom, the Dalai Lama has noted that he was not necessarily a better student than his brother. He believes that the monks whipped his brother to scare him, the fledgling Dalai Lama, into compliance.

Despite the luxuries of monastic life and the easy availability of companionship, Jamphel Yeshe keenly felt the separation from his family. His brother was sent away to private school when the Dalai Lama was only eight years old. Thereafter, the siblings only saw each other at school holidays. Visits by Jamphel Yeshe's were equally rare.

Jamphel Yeshe's education was modeled on the curriculum for a doctorate in Buddhist belief. On a typical school day, he would arise at 6 a.m., breakfast on a simple meal of tsampa and tea, and then begin his lessons. Once he had mastered the basics of reading, he was taught to write in the formal Tibetan script known as Ume, the language of government documents. Being a quick study, he taught himself the more informal and creative Uchen script on the fly. These classes in penmanship gave way to lessons in Buddhism, which generally involved the memorization and recital of a daily text.

The young Dalai Lama's education also included attending a daily meeting with government officials, where he learned by observation and listening.

In the afternoons, he studied logic, art and culture, Sanskrit, medicine, Buddhist philosophy, poetry, meter, synonyms, music, theater, and astrology. The Lama himself considers his early education a poor preparation for his temporal leadership, which would extend into the twenty-first century. In particular, he judges the monastic curriculum as conspicuously lacking in science and medicine.

The very young Jamphel Yeshe was, in some ways, a classic underachiever. He was smart and quick but, by his own admission, did the minimum needed to stay out of trouble. Buddhist students were evaluated largely by their success in oral testing, framed as debates. During these debates, teachers pose a question and the student is judged, not just by his knowledge but also by his wit, mental agility, and ability to win an argument. A high-performing student is one who can get the better of his teacher in a debate. Buddhist debates are so lively that they often blur the line between education and entertainment. During the Dalai Lama's childhood, many students were tested in public, and debates often drew a crowd of spectators, similar to those for street performances. As he grew, the fourteenth Dalai Lama excelled at these events and even bested some of the faith's top scholars. Nevertheless, he thinks his education suffered from a lack of peer competition.

Jamphel Yeshe's lessons always began after breakfast and, save for a two-hour break in the afternoon, went until 5:30 p.m.. It may sound like a grueling schedule for a young boy, but within the rigor of this day, the Lama still found time to observe the red-beaked blackbirds on the palace balcony and the mice that fed on the candle wax in his room. His daydreams were assisted by a rooftop telescope, which he used in the early evenings to spy on the nearby villagers of Shol.

He also found time for organized play. When the sun was at its height at noon, and in the late afternoons between the end of lessons and dinner, the young Lama was allowed free use of his vivid imagination. The games he played betray that he was a child first and Dalai Lama only second. He had a set of toy soldiers that he deployed in elaborate war games. Later, he would melt them down and recast them as peace-advocating monks, but as a child he adored fantasy conflict and epic toy battles. He also made models of airplanes and army tanks using dough made from barley (the same tsampa upon which he breakfasted). And he conscripted his servants into joining him and making models of their own, which he would then critique—often scathingly. At times, to avoid the scorn of a six-year-old world leader, the servants resorted to buying the models the Lama had made. The currency used in these transactions was tsampa dough, and the Lama often turned a brisk profit.

Meals at the palace—even for the head-of-state elect—were extremely simple affairs. If breakfast was little more than a barley paste, dinners were similarly spartan and consisted of tea, weak soup, and yoghurt. The centerpiece of the meal was fresh-baked bread, prepared by the Lama's mother and delivered every week to the palace. Meat was scarce when it was present at all. Buddhism does not forbid the consumption of meat or the purchase of meat, but it does forbid practitioners to kill animals or hire others to do so. Back in Taktser, any meat on the Lama's family's table would probably have been butchered and sold by Muslims. In an isolated, all-Buddhist community like the Dalai Lama's palaces, meat was inevitably scarce. Despite the simplicity of his meals, the cold weather that characterizes Tibet's extreme altitudes, and a somewhat rigorous academic schedule, the Dalai Lama looks back on his years of monastic training with tenderness and yearning.

Little did the young Lama know that his days in Tibet would be numbered. When he was a child of ten, eleven, and twelve years, it would have seemed that his life was a forgone conclusion. He would finish his education, begin his leadership of Tibet's spiritual and secular realms, and bask in his countrymen's love and adoration until his death. How could he possibly know that, at fifteen, he would be forced to assume an authority for which he was not yet prepared? How could he know that he would be forced to flee Tibet in fear of his life when he was still a young man?

The young Dalai Lama's education did not offer much insight into the growing body of science and technology that would ineradicably change the landscape of the twentieth and twenty-first centuries. Nor did he learn much about the world beyond the high mountain ranges that buffer Tibet. But among the various belongings left behind by the thirteenth Dalai Lama, Jamphel Yeshe found a couple of hand-operated movie projectors and a few reels of film. None of the Buddhist intellectuals surrounding him knew how to make these implements work, but the Lama's fascination was so intense that an elderly Chinese monk, handy with technology, was located to get the projectors up and running. This was Jamphel Yeshe's first and, for quite some time, only education in applied science.

The Dalai Lama's fascination with film led him to dream of making his own film at the age of thirteen. It was this dream that put him in contact with Heinrich Harrer, the Austrian immigrant who would later write *Seven Years in Tibet* about his friendship with the Dalai Lama. Harrer had escaped from a British detention camp and, using advanced mountain-climbing skills, made his way into central Tibet, where he was hired to translate foreign news and take photographs for the Tibetan government. In his spare time, he taught the Tibetans how to ice skate, a recreation that became quite popular in a land locked in by mountains and plagued by long winters. In this role as technical expert, Harrer was summoned to the Dalai Lama's palace in Portala, for Jamphel Yeshe dreamt of making a film about ice skating.

Harrer met the Dalai Lama's enthusiasm for modern technology with the expertise to make it happen. The man built a movie theater for the young leader and rigged it up to a

Jeep engine to make it run. Thereafter, Harrer became Jamphel Yeshe's tutor in English, geography, and science, fields of study that the young Dalai Lama sensed were lamentably absent from his lessons with the monks. Harrer and Jamphel Yeshe thus founded a friendship that would last all their lives.

When he was finally able to see the films he had inherited from the former Dalai Lama, Jamphel Yeshe discovered that one recorded the coronation of King George V. Another film was a documentary of the dangers of gold mining while the final film was a dance fantasy. It was a small window on the greater world that lay far beyond Tibet, but it was perhaps the first step in a life journey that would eventually take him to all corners of the world.

Invasion

In 1948, China sent spies into Tibet to learn the strength of its military and whether it was allied with any powerful world forces that would protect it against a Chinese invasion. What the Chinese learned gave them a great deal of confidence. The Tibetan army was only 8,500 men strong, and its armaments had not kept pace with the modern world. There were enough rifles to arm Tibetan fighters, but the country only possessed 200 machine guns and 250 mortars. This skeletal force was little more than a domestic police department, strong enough to deter individual personas non grata that might attempt to cross into Tibet and to keep order among the normally peaceful Tibetans but not powerful enough to repel a full-scale invasion.

And Tibet underwent a civil conflict that further depleted its fighting resources, rendering it even more vulnerable to China's expansionist goals. The Dalai Lama was an early teenager when rival factions went to war over the regency of Tibet. A government led by reincarnated Dalai Lamas inevitably relied on interim leadership by a regent, who typically governed for eighteen to twenty years between the death of one Dalai Lama and the maturity of the next. During any Dalai Lama's childhood, the regent was the effective monarch of Tibet. The regency, therefore, was a coveted position.

The regent at that time, Reting Rinpoche, who had identified the two-year old Lhamo Dhondup as the future head of Buddhism, had a dual role as interim head of state and the lead tutor to the new Dalai Lama. However, Reting Rinpoche was under a cloud of suspicion. Gossip had it that he had breached his vows of celibacy and acted vindictively by punishing one of his critics. When the fourteenth Dalai Lama was only six years old, Reting Rinpoche resigned his position. Despite being only six years old, Jamphe Yeshe was asked to name a new regent and head tutor, so he promoted one of his other tutors, Tathag Rinpoche, to the position.

But the reign of Tathag Rinpoche soon appeared to be as corrupt as that of his predecessor. As a consequence, the former regent Reting Rinpoche saw an opportunity to launch a coup and regain his former position. A civil conflict ensued, causing considerable bloodshed and the loss of Tibet's defensive military power. Reting Rinpoche ultimately failed and subsequently died in prison. This civil struggle unfortunately coincided with the ascension of the People's Republic of China under Chairman Mao Tse Tung.

When Tibet's government learned of China's reconnaissance, the country sent telegrams to Great Britain, India, and the United States of America, asking that they help defend Tibet from China. These telegrams requested an invitation to parlay. Tibet hoped to send a delegation to each country to negotiate in person for aid. They never got that far, however, because each country politely declined to receive a delegation from Tibet.

It is worth pausing in our story to consider why China felt so strongly that Tibet should be annexed and why no major world power came to the rescue. China believed—and believes to this day—that Tibet is a province or feudal state belonging to China by right. Until 1910, this relationship had been mostly symbolic. Tibet, protected by a ring of mountains, kept to itself, governed itself, and resolved its own domestic matters.

China's claim to Tibet was not universally recognized. The thirteenth Dalai Lama, Thubten Gyatso, strongly resented Tibet's nominal subordination to China and took considerable measures to end the relationship. In 1904, he traveled to Mongolia where, in meetings with local leadership, he declared his intention to sever ties with China. Later, he met with Chinese Emperor Guangxu, leader of the Qing dynasty. Guangxu attempted to compel the thirteenth Dalai Lama to recognize China's authority in Tibet, but Thubten Gyatso asserted his belief in Tibet's independence by refusing to submit.

In 1906, however, the Chinese made a move that would eventually render the conquest of Tibet much easier. In exchange for a substantial payment from the Qing government, Great Britain signed a treaty with China, agreeing not to interfere with China's "administration" of Tibet. It was essentially a bribe, but it tied Britain's hands when Tibet later asked for help.

In 1910, Emperor Guangxu sent troops into Tibet, driven by the thirteenth Dalai Lama's refusal to recognize Tibet's subordination to China. The Chinese Emperor officially deposed the Dalai Lama, though this demotion had no practical effect within the borders of Tibet. Dalai Lama Thubten Gyatso fled to India during this invasion, setting a precedent for his next incarnation. Thubten Gyatso's stay in India was short-lived, however. The overthrow of the Qing dynasty in China facilitated the peaceful withdrawal of

Chinese troops from Tibet, and the thirteenth Dalai Lama returned to Tibet in 1912. The new Chinese government made futile overtures to the thirteenth Dalai Lama, offering to "restore" to him an authority that the Tibetans knew he had never lost. Thubten Gyatso's reply was again definitive: he had no interest in any Chinese titles or symbolic authority. He was the absolute political and spiritual authority in Tibet, and he sought no further power.

Upon returning to Tibet, Thubten Gyatso declared the nation independent. He assigned the country an official flag and issued the country's first Tibetan paper currency and postage stamps. Thubten Gyatso knew that these gestures would make little difference in the ethnic and religious identity of the average Tibetans, as they saw themselves—as they had for centuries—as culturally and racially distinct from the Chinese. Instead, the nationalistic fervor was directed at other countries. By creating those tokens, Thuben Gyatso asserted that Tibet was an independent, self-governing nation. Unfortunately, these gestures did not go far enough. Thubten Gyatso was politically astute enough to realize that his belief in Tibet's autonomy was insufficient to protect it, but apparently not astute enough to realize that further action should be taken to make the rest of the world recognize

Tibet's autonomy. For some reason, he did not petition for Tibet to join the United Nations or the League of Nations, nor did he appoint any overseas ambassadors.

These omissions have haunted the fourteenth Dalai Lama for decades. The absence of these important milestones of independence may have been a deciding factor in China's subsequent complete subjugation of Tibet.

When China invaded Tibet in 1949, they managed to spin their invasion as a decision to "liberate" Tibet from imperialist domination. During the subsequent and frequent Tibetan uprisings against Chinese occupation, Chinese broadcasts incessantly repeated the notion that Tibet was under the hypnotic spell of another malevolent foreign power. From the Chinese point of view, this accusation may have held some meaning. Tibet had, from time to time, opened friendly negotiations with India and Great Britain. From the Tibetan point of view, however, the Chinese insistence that Tibet was in the thrall of a foreign power was psychotic nonsense. What imperialist domination? The roadless mountain ranges around Tibet meant that only the hardiest mountaineers, arriving by foot or on horseback, had even a chance of crossing the border. An immigrant to Tibet was such a rarity that many Tibetans had never seen one. Until 1950, Tibet was so isolated that many people think it was the inspiration for many of the Shangri-La and lost paradise stories. In his autobiography, the Dalia Lama often notes that the only imperialist powers in Tibet were the Chinese themselves.

Why did the Chinese want Tibet? It was not a conspicuously wealthy nation, nor had it achieved any important scientific advancements that would be coveted by invaders. But Tibet did possess huge tracts of undeveloped and uninhabited land. Tibet's population was mostly stable, which allowed it to preserve these open spaces. But in China, overpopulation was rampant. Even in 1950, the Chinese were already running out of space. So they needed Tibet principally for the extra land it offered their expanding population. In addition to that, Tibet had many untapped mineral resources and ancient forests, untouched because of the Buddhist respect for trees and wildlife.

When the Chinese began their invasion of Tibet, Tibet's appeal for help from other world powers mostly fell on deaf ears. The leadership of India lodged a formal written protest, but China responded sharply, essentially telling India not to meddle, and India complied in fear of China's superior military power.

After an initial stand in Denkok, where highly-trained Tibetan warriors briefly held off the intruders, Tibet fell to China with little resistance. In 1951, the Chinese army marched on Lhasa, the capital and home of the Dalai Lama.

As it became obvious that the Chinese would triumph, a consensus emerged that the Dalai Lama, only fifteen, should immediately be put in charge of the country. By tradition, the Dalai Lama would have assumed authority at the age of eighteen, but Tibet's top leaders believed, with some justice, that, even at the tender and inexperienced age of fifteen, the Dalai Lama was the only universally respected and beloved authority figure capable of rallying a country under attack. An oracle was consulted and, in the midst of his ceremonial trance, the oracle declared that Jamphel Yeshe should be immediately promoted to the full authority with which he would otherwise have been vested only in three years. Even as Chinese armies were marching on Tibet's capital, Lhasa's leaders celebrated the Dalai Lama's ascension by declaring an amnesty. All prisoners being held in Tibet's jails were freed.

To counter the Chinese invasion, the Dalai Lama consistently advocated a peaceful, non-violent solution, repeatedly imploring his people not to retaliate even when the Chinese enacted violence. This was construed, even by some Tibetans, as a policy of appeasement and compromise. However, the Dalai Lama's refusal to engage in armed combat had two motivations. The first was his Buddhist training, which taught that the present, corporeal life is of little significance, and that one's future lives will be tainted by demonstrations of violence. Secondly, and perhaps more practically, Tibet was badly outgunned, and any focused resistance would have resulted in an all-out massacre of Tibetans. The proud, independent Tibetans, however, often disobeyed the Dalai Lama and took up arms against the Chinese in sporadic uprisings that occurred throughout the ensuing decades. These uprisings always resulted in the death and further subjugation of the Tibetan people.

The Dalai Lama began his peaceful negotiations by sending a letter to China, admitting that the relationship between the two countries was strained and stating his intention to restore a mutually beneficial friendship. And he asked China politely to withdraw its troops. Shortly thereafter, the Dalai Lama took the precaution of sending some of his treasure to India for safekeeping. A large quantity of gold dust and silver bars made its way from Lhasa to Sikkim, where it remained untouched for nine years.

After that, the Dalai Lama sent a delegation to Peking, China, to negotiate for peace. His goal was to achieve a compromise wherein Tibet would be self-governing but would defer to China on foreign policy. However, that delegation returned to Tibet with a "Seventeen Point Agreement for the Peaceful Liberation of Tibet," a document that the Tibetan delegation had had no hand in writing. The tenor of the agreement was that Tibet was part of China. Once the delegation members had arrived in China, they were held captive and treated like prisoners. They signed the document under compulsion but declined to seal it. This offered no real obstacle to the Chinese, who simply forged the official Tibet seal.

The Seventeen Point Agreement was a draconian document, the language of which mirrored People's Liberation Army propaganda. Moreover, it was obvious from the first that the Chinese had no intention of respecting the points relevant to Tibet's welfare. For instance, the agreement stated that Tibet's religions would not be persecuted and specifically mentioned that monasteries and their monks would be respected, but this was hardly the case. The agreement specified that the Tibetan people's livelihood would be improved, but in fact the

Chinese invasion brought a wave of poverty and food shortages to Tibet.

The Dalai Lama learned that his delegation had signed the agreement when he heard about it over the radio. Soon after that, the Dalai Lama had his first meeting with Chinese officials. As a child, he had loved to spy from rooftops, so it is little wonder that he watched the Chinese officials as they approached the monastery in Yatung where the meeting would take place. The Dalai Lama was underwhelmed by the drab gray suits and gray caps of the first Chinese persons on whom he had ever laid eyes. He had been surrounded, for most of his life, by monks wearing gaudy red and saffron robes. Looking back, the Dalai Lama notes that the dull attire of those approaching Chinamen was a warning that they would soon attempt to make Tibet an equally gray and conforming territory.

The Dalai Lama's meeting with General Chang Chin-wu was uneventful. He presented a letter from Chairman Mao Tse Tung, welcoming Tibet to the motherland. A few months later, 14,000 Chinese soldiers marched into Lhasa, demanding to be fed with local farm products that had been barely sufficient to feed the Tibetans themselves. And so began a reign of terror that was accomplished, in large part, by starving the natives and destroying the country's delicate economy.

The Chinese strategy in Tibet was to appoint a few Tibetans to enforce Chinese rule, even when it was abusive and irrational, thus turning Tibetan authorities against their own people. Whenever Tibetans pushed back against Chinese oppression, the Chinese instructed Tibetan leaders to suppress the opposition. It was a clever tactic, designed to convince the ordinary people of Tibet that their own leaders were in league with the Chinese. China doubtlessly predicted that a people so demoralized would soon submit and accept communism as a relative, if not an absolute, good.

Thus, when Tibetans composed satirical songs about the Chinese and sang them loudly in the streets, the Chinese ordered the token Tibetan government to outlaw singing in the public rights of way. So, with great sadness, the Dalai Lama asked his prime ministers to resign from government to save them from the indignity of coercing their own people against their own judgment.

In China

In 1954, the Dalai Lama, accompanied by high-ranking lama Chökyi Gyaltsen, traveled to China to meet with Mao and to attend the National People's Congress, of which the Dalai Lama had been elected a representative. It was a long and arduous journey that began with the Dalai Lama being driven over roads built by the Chinese with land seized from Tibetan farmers. Then, when they reached the end of the road, they rode horses through dangerous mountains fraught with mudslides and randomly falling boulders. Multiple horses and mules died on the journey, and three people were killed by road hazards. When they again came to car-accessible roads, they mounted jeeps that took them to Chengtu. From Chengtu, they caught a flight and then a train, finally arriving in Peking.

Jamphel Yeshe was treated with every courtesy on this trip; he was given official tours and named deputy chairman of the Standing Committee of the National People's Congress. However, he quickly noticed that he was subject to invisible golden handcuffs. He was frequently invited to sit down and talk with other foreign nationals, but he was never allowed to do so without a Chinese escort, usually one who took notes on everything he said.

Despite token gestures of respect and kindness, he felt that Mao was not sincere in his commitment to finding a solution to the problems that China had introduced to Tibet. Mao's interactions with the Dalai Lama were a mixture of superficial politeness and flashes of contempt. At one point, Mao informed Jamphel Yeshe that religion was "poison." On another occasion, the Dalai Lama invited a number of Chinese officials to participate in a Tibetan ceremony that involved throwing part of a cake up to the ceiling in honor of Buddha. Mao threw a piece of cake at the ceiling. Then, smirking, he threw another piece on the floor.

One thing in which the Chinese expressed great interest was the treasure that the Dalai Lama had sent to India. The Dalai Lama told them, truthfully, that he was considering ordering its return to Tibet. However, he never did retrieve that small fortune, and it served his countrymen well in the next decade.

As for the National People's Congress, to which the Dalai Lama had been appointed, it was quickly apparent that his role was purely decorative. All the proceedings were in Chinese, with no translations offered. Even without a translator, however, Jamphel Yeshe quickly noticed a pattern to these meetings. No diversity of opinions was expressed, nor were any reforms suggested. Meetings were largely devoted to long-winded affirmations of the glories of Chinese Communism. Jamphel Yeshe could not help noticing that even the Chinese delegates seemed bored, as if their only motivation was the thought of the next tea break.

In his travels through rural China, Jamphel Yeshe garnered similar impressions. Achievements in industrialization and better agricultural practices had been won at the cost of a brainwashed people who rarely even laughed without a formal cue from a Communist leader. Nobody burst into song as they hoed a field. The citizenry had sacrificed their individuality and most of their joy to the altar of Communist conformity. They received their news from heavily censored, government-owned newspapers and broadcasts that provided little more than another round of Chinese propaganda. And they all dressed in the same colorless clothing.

Despite these grim portents, the Dalai Lama was erroneously optimistic that his visit would provide some relief to his people back in Tibet. He took Chairman Mao at his word when the latter promised that Tibet would be self-governing. Although Tibet was currently being ordered around by the Chinese military, Mao had promised that a committee would be formed to govern the nation and that a majority of the committee members would be Tibetans.

This committee turned out to be a farce. The Chinese approach to a self-governing Tibet was to appoint a majority of Communist-friendly people to the committee. Using this approach, they were able to create a government with a controlling block of voters who would always parrot the party line.

On his way home to Lhasa, the Dalai Lama stopped off at his birthplace, the tiny village of Taktser. There, with tears in their eyes, villagers told him how grateful they were to Chairman Mao and the great Communist People's Party. He realized with horror that the stifling of diversity and freedom of expression had already begun.

Under Occupation

The Dalai Lama, perhaps with some naiveté, believed for many months that he could hold the Chinese to at least some of the tenets of the Seventeen Point Agreement. He was suspicious enough of the Chinese, however, that he petitioned India for asylum only two years later. But India declined his request, largely because of India's fear of China. Only earlier that same year, India had signed a treaty with China in which India had agreed not to interfere in Chinese affairs.

Meanwhile, China's stated intentions differed wildly from its actions in Tibet. Officially, China occupied Tibet to end a stagnant and old-fashioned monarchic government and to modernize the country by building roads and other infrastructure. However, it was soon clear that the Chinese were in Tibet to exploit its resources. The Chinese mined Tibet's minerals and clear-cut its forests, exporting all of the products back to China. Whereas Tibetan wildlife had been respected and its habitat conserved, the Chinese had no compunction about laying waste and displacing species. Thousands of Chinese soldiers poured into Tibet, putting such a strain on food supplies that famine resulted. China had no use for Tibet's unique language, customs, or religion and sought to erode all of Tibet's cultural distinctions. China was intent on erasing a heritage that had evolved more or less in isolation because of its surrounding mountain ranges. Mass poverty was on the rise. In a country where crime had been mostly unknown, huge prisons were built, mostly to house any Tibetans who resisted Chinese rule.

By 1956, having appealed unsuccessfully to the United Nations and India, the Dalai Lama was desperate enough to accept assistance from the United States Central Intelligence Agency (CIA), although he would later repudiate that relationship. The CIA assisted a rebellion in Kham, a region of China heavily populated by Tibetans. The Agency created a covert military academy in Colorado, called Camp Hale, to train Khampa guerrillas—traditional Tibetan warriors—to fight the Chinese Communists. This CIA contingent attacked the Chinese in Amdo and Kham, where farm owners had been forced to relinquish their property for government redistribution. The Chinese crushed this conflict with the help of Muslim mercenaries, but it gave way to the larger 1959 Tibetan uprising.

In Lhasa, where the Dalai Lama lived, an underground resistance against Chinese occupation developed and grew strong, informally electing its own leaders. When these people led insurrections, the Dalai Lama found himself reduced to the role of damage control. He issued more statements asking people to be patient, non-violent, and cooperative with the Chinese so that the Chinese would not implement their own punishments. The Dalai Lama worried that, by pursuing this course of compromise, he was encouraging his people to think he had sold out. However, history shows that the people of Tibet never blamed Jamphel Yeshe, and they remain loyal to him to this day. It is likely that they saw him for what he was, a man desperately using what little leadership power he still had to protect innocent people from Chinese brutality.

What happened in Chamdo in 1956 provides a microcosmic sample of the Chinese leadership of Tibet. While still under military rule, this eastern province of Tibet became a hotbed of resistance and fighting. A Chinese general met with 350 of the Tibetan leaders and presented them with two alternatives: they could accept Chinese "reforms" immediately, or the reforms could be introduced gradually and only upon approval by a majority of native Tibetans. The latter approach to reforms, the general noted, was the one officially approved by the Dalai Lama. It appears that the Tibetans were not as naive as the Chinese thought. It had not taken them long to see through the Chinese rhetoric of "reform." The leaders of Chamdo availed themselves of a write-in option. Two hundred of the assembled leaders voted never to have any Chinese reforms. This incident clearly showed that the people did not blindly follow the Dalai Lama's leadership, nor did they truly believe that he had aligned himself with the Chinese. Despite this clear majority message, the general thanked the assembly for their input and explained that reforms would begin at once.

It's difficult to imagine a race of people less interested in what the People's Republic of China had to offer than the Tibetans were. Whereas Communist crackdowns in rural China produced a compliant, if joyless, population of farmers, crackdowns in rural Tibet produced a contingent of homeless guerrilla fighters, forever consigned to camp out in Tibet's mountain forests, where they were estranged from their friends and families.

As a follow-up to the mock-democratic process in Chamdo, the Chinese summoned the province's leaders to a fort called Jomdha Dzong. There, the Tibetans were essentially held captive until they agreed to return to their people and enact "reforms." The Tibetans were reduced to bald-faced lying. They agreed to coerce their people into submission, and evidently the Chinese believed them and let their guard down because two hundred Tibetans were able to escape from the fort and flee into the mountains. For fear of reprisal, they never returned to their homes. Instead, they started a regime of guerilla attacks and raids on the Chinese. Eventually, other disenfranchised Tibetan men joined them in the wilderness. As the guerrilla movement grew to dangerous proportions, the Chinese retaliated by bombing their mountain hideouts and the villages where their families remained.

Escape to India

The Dalai Lama's attempts to negotiate a better peace with China had failed, and he began to fear for his freedom if not his life. In March 1959, rebellions against Chinese rule were active in Lhasa, Kham, and Jamphel Yeshe's native Amdo, but it was the love that Tibetans almost universally felt for the Dalai Lama that escalated the Lhasa uprising into outright war.

In the midst of this political chaos, the Dalai Lama was pursuing a lharampa geshe degree, a prestigious credential in Gelug Buddhism. The degree was more or less equivalent to a doctorate. Upon his graduation, he was scheduled to attend a religious celebration in Lhasa, but he received a communique from the Chinese government that demanded his presence at a play taking place in a Chinese military installation. Chinese officers approached the Dalai Lama's bodyguards and informed them that only two men would be allowed to escort Jamphel Yeshe to the play—and that those escorts must be unarmed. The absence of a substantial escort and ceremony surrounding the movements of the Dalai Lama went strongly against Tibetan traditions, but even more threatening was the Chinese injunction that the Dalai Lama's sojourn to the theatre be kept secret.

The Lhasa Tibetans saw this "invitation" as a threat, and they feared that the Dalai Lama would be seized and held captive. Whether the Chinese truly intended to kidnap the Dalai Lama remains uncertain, but the fear of Chinese motives set into motion a chain of events that has changed the history of Tibet and Buddhism.

There were several clues that the Chinese invitation might have been masking an intention to abduct or even murder the Dalai Lama. Another meeting of the Chinese National Assembly was about to take place, and Tibet got wind of a Chinese announcement that the Dalai Lama would attend this event in Peking. Even more alarming was the fact that the Chinese had abducted four high-ranking monks, who had been lured into a trap by way of a similar "invitation." Three of them had been murdered, and the other was incarcerated.

Armed with little more than sticks and knives, several thousand Tibetans surrounded the Dalai Lama's summer palace in Norbulingka, openly declaring their intention to prevent him from leaving the palace. They began a chant, demanding that the Chinese leave Tibet. Simultaneously, protests broke out in the streets of Lhasa. Meetings were held, and street demonstrations expressed a bitter resentment against Chinese interference. Tibetan soldiers who had been conscripted into the Chinese army discarded their Chinese uniforms and donned their traditional Tibetan gear.

The Dalai Lama was, at this point, essentially a prisoner in his own home, hemmed in both by contemptuous Chinese warlords and by throngs of loyal followers who believed they were protecting him. He soon became worried—and justifiably so— that the Chinese would enact terrible violence against the people surrounding the palace. He pled with the people surrounding his palace to disband, but they ignored him. As Chinese troops formed an outer ring around the band of Tibetans at the palace, it became clear that they were prepared to take violent military action to regain control of the situation.

During the days that followed, the Dalai Lama exchanged several letters with the Chinese. Hoping to mitigate the Chinese wrath, he was reduced to lying. His first letter apologized for the behavior of the Tibetans and expressed his regret that he had not been able to attend the play to which he had been invited. In the second letter, he agreed that the people assembled outside the palace were hurting the relationship between Tibet and China. The third letter stated his intention to sort out which Tibetans were willing to embrace China's new policies from those who were not.

The Dalai Lama wrote these letters in response to correspondence he received from Chinese General Tan Kuan-sen. During the siege of Norbulinka, Jamphel Yeshe also received a letter from Ngapoi Ngawang Jigme, a Tibetan who had turned himself into a puppet of the Chinese invaders and been awarded a high position in government. This letter announced that the Chinese had imminent plans to attack the palace and asked the Dalai Lama to specify which part of the palace he would be in, so that the Chinese would not kill him in the process of destroying the rest of the building.

After the Dalai Lama fled to India, the Chinese published the letters he wrote to General Tan Kuan-sen. Having been carefully removed from their context, these letters became a device by which the Chinese attempted to persuade the world that the Dalai Lama had sincerely sought protection against his own people. And the Chinese were, to some extent, successful with this ruse. The letters did in fact persuade many people to believe that the Dalai Lama had fled Tibet in fear of the Tibetans, not of the Chinese. In a formal

Parliamentary meeting a year later, an English lord quoted the Dalai Lama's letter and framed it in that context.

The Dalai Lama claims that, at no point during these proceedings, even when the Chinese were preparing to shell his palace, was he afraid to die. His Buddhist training placed him in good stead and insulated him from the panic that another man might have felt under the same circumstances. And one piece of evidence particularly compels us to believe him: all of the letters sent to the Chinese by the besieged Dalai Lama have become a part of history's public record, yet in not one of those letters did he reveal his location within the palace.

On March 17, two artillery shells exploded near the palace, and two days later the Chinese began their attack in earnest.

Leaving Lhasa at a time when his leadership was needed was not an easy decision for the Dalai Lama. He consulted an oracle for advice, and the oracle's message was not in the least ambiguous. Not only did he emphatically state that the Dalai Lama should flee, but he also produced a map and drew a route out of Tibet.

With much trepidation, Jamphel Yeshe decided that it was time to leave. He removed his glasses, believing that nobody would recognize him without them. He also disguised himself in secular clothing, slung a rifle over his shoulder, and walked out of his palace, using the cover of a convenient dust storm to evade notice of the surrounding Chinese troops. His mother, his youngest brother, and an older sister had been visiting him in Norbulinka before the uprising, so of necessity they traveled with him. The Dalai Lama's escape retinue left the palace in small groups, reuniting once they were safely away from the palace. They then rode away from Norbulingka on an array of animals that included horses, ponies, mules, yaks, and yak hybrids. They traveled under the guard of the Chushi Gangdrug, a band of trained guerilla fighters. It took two days before the Chinese discovered the Dalai Lama's defection, and they swung into action, closing the border to India and sending troops after him. The Dalai Lama's travel party deliberately chose a difficult, unpaved route that took them south and southeast of Lhasa and that leveraged the Tibetan's superior knowledge of the mountain ranges. As they made their way across the mountain passes, the Dalai Lama and his companions were welcomed by the Tibetans of the small mountain villages. Often, small crowds of mountain folk would line the paths to observe their great spiritual leader.

They frequently dismounted their horses and made their way on foot to rest the animals. It was not a purely practical measure; their belief in the teachings of Buddha also led them to respect all animals and treat them with kindness. Despite this, the livestock showed signs of weariness as the journey progressed. At a mountain pass called Che-la, a Tibetan mountain dweller, Tashi Norbu, gifted the Dalai Lama with a beautiful, all-white horse. This raised the spirits of the weary travelers, for such a gift was a good omen.

The Dalai Lama did not originally intend to leave Tibet. When he had fled the palace, his original intention was simply to escape Lhasa and the clutch of the Chinese military. He and his escape party had planned to stop at Lhuntse Dzong, a Tibetan village near the border to India, and continue negotiating for relief from Chinese oppression. But the escape party had brought battery-operated radios, so they were able to hear news broadcasts from Voice of America. What they heard horrified them. Despite the fact that the Dalai Lama had left his palace, the Chinese had bombed it anyway, and thousands of Tibetans were lying dead in the streets. The people surrounding the palace had been massacred, and much of the palace had been destroyed. The Chinese did not stop there, continuing their destruction at the Dalai Lama's winter palace in Potala. There they attacked and destroyed a government school, a medical college, the burial site of the thirteenth Dalai Lama, and the homes of private individuals living in Shol, the village at the foot of the palace. The Chinese shelled Lhasa wantonly and also attacked monasteries.

As word of these Chinese reprisals reached him, the Dalai Lama's goal changed and the escape party made for India. They concluded that the Chinese would retaliate against anyone who offered harbor or protection to the Dalai Lama and that, to prevent such bloodshed, he must leave the country.

Their journey became even more difficult as they followed a path blazed by mountain traders. They made their way over mountain passes that sometime rose as high as 19,000 feet above sea level. Where the snow had melted, the resulting mud was slippery and dangerous. The facial hair of men who had been unable to stop for a shave filled up with ice. They contended not only with cold but also with blinding sunlight, and few of the travelers had sun goggles. The others wound strips of cloth, or in some cases their own hair, across their eyes to protect them.

The villages along the way had few resources for sheltering such a prestigious band of refugees. When they reached the humble town of E-Chhudhogyang, they spent the night in cattle pens. Soon after that, they learned that the Chinese had dismantled the puppet government that had purported to offer Tibet autonomous self-rule. The country was, once again, under the thumb of a vicious military.

Finally, at Mangmang, the last Tibetan village in Tibet, the Dalai Lama fell sick. He was unable to get back on his horse. A day later, he could hardly move. Meanwhile, the escape party heard a radio broadcast that announced that the Dalai Lama had fallen off his horse. Jamphel Yeshe, ever sensitive to situational irony, smiled to himself. It was the one hardships that had not befallen him.

The refugees were stuck in Mangmang for two days. The Dalai Lama was far too ill to ride a horse, but they feared that a further delay would allow the Chinese to catch up with them. So they put the Dalai Lama on top of a hardy dzomo—half cow and half yak. The Dalai Lama was familiar with dzomo, as they were among the livestock kept by his father in Taktser, the village of his birth. The dzomo's broad back and steady, even stride made it possible for the Dalai Lama to continue his journey, and it was on the back of that humble animal that he left his beloved Tibet and crossed over into India, the country he would call home for the next 55 years.

Tibet in Exile

The Dalai Lama's escape made world news, and suddenly Tibet and its problems were on the map. United States President Dwight Eisenhower got caught up in the suspense and put a trail of pins in a map tracing the Lama's escape. Newspaper journalists called it the "story of the year."

The journey across the mountains into India took two weeks. Meanwhile, in the United States, Central Intelligence Agency operative John Greaney sent a cable to India asking, on behalf of the U.S., that the Dalai Lama be given sanctuary in India. To what extent the CIA directive influenced India's actions is unclear; India had been disposed, of its own volition, to sympathize with Tibet's plight. What we do know is that Jamphel Yeshe was immediately offered asylum by Prime Minister Jawaharlal Nehru, who sent Indian troops to meet him at the border and lead him to the Tawang monastery. Eventually, Jamphel Yeshe settled in Dharamsala.

One of the Dalai Lama's first actions upon resettling in India was to repudiate the Seventeen Point Agreement that Tibet had signed with China. He declared that the contract was null and void because China had breached its tenets.

The Dalai Lama had received little training in politics and none in international law, so upon his arrival in India, he spent much of his time consulting with international experts and agents, among them the International Commission of Jurists.

The International Commission of Jurists (ICJ) was—and still is—a non-governmental organization with a standing membership of judges, lawyers, and scholars who advocate for international human rights and the rule of law. The ICJ had been formed just seven years earlier to investigate and report on human rights abuses in Soviet-controlled East Germany. The ICJ took a keen interest in the problems of Tibet. The commission conducted a study and concluded that the combined abuses of the Tibetan people amounted to nothing short of genocide. In making this pronouncement, they looked not only at the number of Tibetans who had been killed or had disappeared but also at the brutal public executions, some of them involving scalding and disembowelment. They also considered the reports of children stolen from their parents, children being forced to kill their own parents, and monks who were subjected to a slow death while being told that they should ask their gods for salvation. These were only a few of

China's human rights abuses in Tibet, reports of which were flooding into India upon the Dalai Lama's arrival.

The Dalai Lama's flight from Tibet angered the people, who loved and admired their young leader, and led to a short but bloody rebellion, which was soon settled in favor of the Chinese. Meanwhile, beginning in 1959, thousands of abused and mistreated Tibetans made the precarious trek over the mountain ranges to join Jamphel Yeshe in India and escape Chinese persecution. A high percentage of monks and nuns made up this emigrant Tibetan community, but farmers, families, and high-ranking government officials also sought refuge. Many of them died crossing the mountains, and many more died when they arrived in India because they were unable to adapt to the hot weather and low altitude. In addition, Tibet had been mostly free of diseases, so with no built-up immunity, many of the emigrants succumbed to tuberculosis and digestive disorders. By the time India was hosting 30,000 Tibetan refugees, the Dalai Lama had—in cooperation with India's prime minister—created jobs for them building roads in India's higher altitudes.

The hardships faced by the adult immigrants to India were terrible, but they were compounded for the children, many of whom died during the trip over the mountains. Many more Tibetan children succumbed to death in India because their immune systems were not yet strong enough to adapt to the changes in climate and the presence of communicable illnesses.

To save the lives of Tibetan children in exile, the Dalai Lama used the small personal fortune he had sent to India for safekeeping nine years earlier. With that money, he set up boarding schools for Tibetan children. The boarding schools provided safe housing, meals, medical care, and education. Assisted by his sister, the Dalai Lama established a curriculum that included the study of Tibetan history and religion, Hindi, and English. But, ever aware of the faults of his own education, the Dalai Lama also made sure that these children were taught math, science, and geography. As such, these schools were poised to protect Tibet's heritage while also preparing young people for emerging careers in the modern world. By starting up these schools, the Dalai Lama accomplished two things. He ensured the health and safety of Tibetan children while also ensuring the perpetuation of Tibetan culture and knowledge through the next generation. Soon after the Dalai Lama announced his plan to provide for the education of Tibetan children in exile, he found himself personally in charge of 800 children. In his autobiography, the Dalai Lama notes that Tibetan children raised within a ruthless program of Communist indoctrination were simply unable to resist assimilation into Chinese communism, so the future of true Tibetan customs and culture lay with the children of Tibetan exiles.

Despite the risks of traveling and the perils that awaited in India, Tibetans continued streaming over the border until there were 80,000 Tibetan refugees living in India. A Central Relief Committee for Tibetan Refugees was formed by the citizens of India. Many nations sent financial aid to address this emergency. South Vietnam sent quantities of rice while Britain, America, Australia, and New Zealand all sent gifts earmarked for educational assistance.

This mass emigration of his people prompted the Dalai Lama to establish the Tibetan government-in-exile. Even today, this government remains unrecognized by most world powers. Despite that, the resulting Central Tibetan Administration (CTA) is probably the main reason why most people in the world have heard of Tibet and understand its plight. The CTA's mission, in addition to protecting the welfare and cultural distinctions of exiled Tibetans, is to liberate Tibet from Chinese oppression through peaceful action and education. The CTA claims no governmental authority in Tibet. It has publically stated that, if the Chinese abdicate, the CTA will voluntarily dissolve and give way to a self-governed Tibet.

Today, the CTA has all the earmarks of a stable democracy. The Dalai Lama created a parliament and instituted elections. A cabinet of ministers, each with a specific area of expertise, advises the Kalon Tripa, who is effectively a prime minister. Within the CTA, ministers were appointed by the Dalai Lama until his resignation from secular leadership. They were allowed to address parliament but not to vote. The Dalai Lama also established a Supreme Court to administer justice. This judicial branch was endowed with the ability to deprive the Dalai Lama of power, should they deem it appropriate. Though that power was never exercised, it was an important step in establishing a system of checks and balances consistent with democracy. With these institutions in place, the Dalai Lama has systematically removed himself from government leadership in stages, focusing more and more on spiritual leadership and enlightenment.

India donated several large tracts of land for the resettlement of the refugees, who eventually became self-sufficient as farmers. The Tibetans had a rough transition to India. In order to farm, they were required to burn trees and clear land, a practice that goes against the deeply-ingrained Buddhist respect for wildlife and natural habitats. These displaced Tibetans were also limited in their agricultural knowledge, having raised little more than barley, buckwheat, and potatoes. With some coaxing by Indian talent, they expanded their repertoire to include corn and fruit trees.

During his first year of exile, he established the Tibetan Institute of Performing Arts to keep alive the traditions of Tibetan dance, theater, opera, and other musical genres. Within the safety of this institution, a Tibetan opera company was born. Day-long performances provided entertainment for Tibetan refugees while reminding them of home.

The vast number of self-exiled Tibetans and the world's growing awareness of Tibet as the global heart of Buddhism gave the Dalai Lama a tool for negotiation that he had previously lacked. During this time, the Dalai Lama's appeals to the United Nations were finally heard. This resulted in the adoption of three resolutions by the UN's General Assembly, in 1959, 1961, and 1965. All three resolutions called for China to restore human rights in Tibet.

1960s: The Fight to Preserve Tibet Tradition

Unfortunately, the United Nations resolutions fell on deaf ears. However, in 1962, the Dalai Lama published his first autobiography, titled *My Land and My People: The Memoirs of His Holiness the Dalai Lama of Tibet.* The book recounted the drama of his life so far—his quiet upbringing in monastic Tibet, the invasion of the Chinese, and their subsequent cruelty to his people, concluding with his flight to India. The book was well-received internationally and did its part to create awareness of the tragedy taking place in Tibet.

Shortly after the Dalai Lama's flight to India, Mao Tse Tung seized absolute control of China and initiated the period of horrors known as the Cultural Revolution. In 1967, this revolution came to Tibet. Any pretense at friendship was dropped, and Chinese soldiers launched a full-scale program to assimilate the Tibetan mind, body, and soul. Centuries-old holy places were torn down, sacred texts were trampled and destroyed, and any monks who resisted were dragged through the streets. The systematic destruction of Tibet's culture was accelerated. The exiled Tibetans living in India, where they were free to practice their traditions, offered the only real hope that Tibetan culture would not be irrevocably lost.

However, in India, the Dalai Lama found ways to save the cultural distinctions that were being crushed by Chinese dominion. In 1967, the same year that Chinese teenagers under the banner of the Cultural Revolution were dismantling Tibetan temples, he created a university-level institution of learning called the Central Institute of Higher Tibetan Studies. Located in Sarnath, Varanasi, India, it was co-founded by Jawaharlal Nehru as an extension of Sampurnanand Sanskrit University. In addition to teaching Tibetan youth in exile, it also educated Tibetan students who lived in the Himalayan border. The Institute still exists, and one of its long-term missions is to translate Buddhist texts that exist only in Sanskrit into modern languages, especially Hindi. This mission is important in creating world awareness of the Buddhist belief system. In 1977, the institute broke off from Sampurnanand Saskrit University and became independent, though it is still supported financially by the Indian government.

The year 1967 was also the year the Dalai Lama began his work as an international spokesperson for peace. His first move in this direction was to visit Japan and Thailand, speak to the monks there, and begin to understand Buddhism in its international context. What he found was that the Buddhist values he had learned in Tibet are more or less the same in the other parts of the world where the religion is practiced.

But the Dalai Lama did not limit his observations to religious practices. In Japan, he was impressed by the country's clear determination to preserve its cultural distinctions while also benefitting from the advances of technology. He also noted an obsession with tidiness such as he had never seen and a concern with food presentation that, he believed, put presentation first and taste second.

In Thailand, he met with King Bhumipol and Prime Minister Thanom Kittikachorn. The Dalai Lama found the Thai heat even more oppressive than that of India, and the mosquitoes annoyed him. Nevertheless, the Thai monks helped him immensely in his quest to put Buddhism in its greater world context.

Whilst on this maiden tour, the Dalai Lama saw a B-52 bomber flying over Vietnam and made the observation that human cruelty had expanded into the skies.

The Dalai Lama's first diplomatic tour would be the last in which he could meet freely with world leaders. China reacted to the news of his foreign visits by proclaiming that any meetings between a foreign leader and the Dalai Lama would be construed as interference with China's internal affairs. That edict remains in place to the present day. This constraint did not slow Jamphel Yeshe's globe-trotting, but it did guarantee that he would have to visit in the guise of a teacher and spiritual advisor and not as a political advocate of any kind.

However, the Dalai Lama has met informally with many world leaders, including United States presidents, often under the escort of a leading religious figure so that the meeting could be billed as spiritual consultation.

1970s: The Dalai Lama Forges the "Middle Way"

In 1970, as a part of his ongoing efforts to save Tibet's culture, the Dalai Lama started the Library of Tibetan Works and Archives. Located in Dharamsala, the library and archive are now home to more than 80,000 manuscripts of critical importance to Tibet's culture, history, religion, and governance. In this library, precious manuscripts that were smuggled out of Tibet on yaks along with the Dalai Lama have found a home. In addition to books, the library also houses Tibetan artifacts such as statues, mandalas, and thangkas, which are elaborate paintings executed on cotton or silk. The third floor of the library came to be officially designated as a museum of Tibetan artifacts, many of which date back to the twelfth century.

In 1973, the Dalai Lama embarked on an ambitious eleven-country tour of Europe. It was his first exposure to the West, a far-off destination that, as a child, he had known only through books and photographs. His first stop was Rome, where upon seeing trees and houses, he immediately concluded that cultural differences are largely superficial. This belief in the underlying brotherhood of all people would blend seamlessly with his message of peace as he carved out his role as an international peace advocate. He met with Pope Paul VI, and they found common ground in their conviction that faith brings meaning to life regardless of the belief system. The Dalai Lama spent too little time in any one country to get more than a superficial look at the culture, but his European tour sparked great interest in Buddhism, the troubles of Tibet, and the institution of the Dalai Lama. More invitations to Europe would follow.

In 1975, the Dalai Lama contended with the publication of something called the Yellow Book. Published two years previously, the Yellow Book celebrated the Gelug Buddhist deity Dorje Shugden, whose main role is to punish Gelug Buddhists who blend their religious practices with other, non-Gelug Buddhist traditions. The Yellow Book is a series of stories in which Dorje Shugden violently punishes those Gelug believers who do not practice an unadulterated version of Gelug Buddhism.

The Dalai Lama, with eyes opened from world travel and meaningful conversations with people of all faiths, could not advocate a hard line that called, in effect, for partisanship within the international Buddhist community. This is a man who had found many commonalities in the teachings of Catholicism and Buddhism. He saw the Yellow Book as divisive and counterproductive. He publicly repudiated Dorje

Shugden and those who favored Gelug separatism, expressing a belief that all Buddhist traditions were of equal value.

The Dalai Lama may have seen his repudiation of Dorje Shugden as a matter of bringing the world's Buddhist community together without divisions, but his public pronouncement had unintended consequences. Followers of Dorje Shugden found themselves unwelcome within the ranks of Buddhists who heeded the Dalai Lama's advice to abjure the controversial god. Within Tibet and within the Indian population of Tibetans in exile, an apartheid of sorts was enacted. Years later, a strong resistance movement would form around the rejected Dorje Shugden.

Back in 1979, however, it was time for the Dalai Lama to visit the United States. "Hello Dalai" was the *New York Times'* glib headline announcing his arrival in the U.S. It was with some fear and trepidation that the Dalai Lama entered the heart of capitalism. Though he had been ever skeptical of China's communist message, he had been inundated for years with the message that capitalism, as represented by the United States, was evil incarnate. Despite that, the Dalai Lama arrived in the U.S. fully prepared to draw his own unbiased conclusions.

His review of the United States was mixed. He greatly admired the freedom that Americans have to express opinions, including controversial and political stances, without fear of retribution. And he found that this freedom extended to lifestyle choices. He was impressed by the warmth and friendliness of the American people. Though he spoke little English, he found that he had many avid listeners.

But in his observation, freedom and individuality were not always good things when taken to an extreme. They could lead to broken families, alienation, and loneliness.

The Dalai Lama was also troubled by the sharp disparities between rich and poor in such an affluent nation. The homelessness and ghettos he observed had no equivalent in Tibet, either before or after the Communist invasion.

On his first trip to America, the Dalai Lama was not yet the household name he would become. He gave his lessons in small theaters and auditoriums that were often only half-full. His trip backers had trouble interesting the media in his visit. When they called a radio or television station to ask if they would like to interview the Dalai Lama, a typical response was, "What did you say her last name was?" It would be a few years before crowds of thousands would jockey for a glimpse of him.

However, the insights he gained from his trips to America and Europe directly shaped the Dalai Lama's political philosophy of "the middle way." The middle way describes a way of life that blends elements of capitalism and communism. A pathway between the two extremes is the most likely road to prosperity and happiness, he believes. The Dalai Lama's belief in this middle way has led to a number of changes in the sphere of his activities. The parliamentary government of the exiled Tibet community has become progressively more democratic.

But the principal application of the middle way has been to the Dalai Lama's negotiations with China. Beginning in 1979, the Dalai Lama ceased to lobby for Tibet's complete liberation from China. His middle way approach recognizes that, in the modern world, nations have become very interdependent. Therefore, he now asks for concessions rather than complete independence. The middle way seeks to make Tibet a zone of peace with its own elected government, religious freedom, a cessation of human rights abuses, and a stop order on the relocation of Han Chinese to Tibet.

In the 1970s, when he was at home in India and not traveling, the Dalai Lama evolved daily habits that have remained largely unchanged up to the present. He rises at 4 a.m. and drinks warm water and a Tibetan medicinal drink. He spends five of the day's hours in prayer. He eats little meat, though his doctors have urged him to desist from absolute vegetarianism after a bout with hepatitis weakened him. He abstains from sex in observance of his monk's vows. He has never married or had children of his own.

The town of Dharamsala was a British outpost during India's colonial period. It is in the foothills of the Himalayas, only 100 miles from the Tibetan border. Snow caps the mountains, and monasteries abound. Despite these resources, it is a poor town, and isolated for lack of a functioning nearby airport. Upon returning from his travels, the Dalai Lama must first fly into Delhi, then endure a ten-hour drive down narrow rural roads that are frequently jammed with pedestrian traffic, bicycles, trucks, and livestock. An army canteen, a small Anglican church, and a scattering of military cottages remain as artifacts of that time. The Dalai Lama and his family settled in McLeod Ganj, a former settlement up the mountain from Dharamsala. It was an empty ghost-town when they arrived, the former inhabitants having been evacuated in 1947 owing to Partition. Since then, a bustling town has arisen around the Dalai Lama. Dharamsala has become an exceptionally popular destination for serious spiritual seekers, and locals do a brisk business providing housing, food, and recreation for these visitors.

In the late 1970s, the Dalai Lama met a man who would become, arguably, his most influential fan. Actor Richard Gere made his way to the Dalai Lama's humble home in Dharamsala to hear the message of Tibetan Buddhism from the horse's mouth. Gere had begun studying Buddhism in his twenties. As a young man, he strongly felt the alienation and purposelessness that life in the modern world can impose. He often worried for his sanity. During this lonely and anxious time in his life, he started haunting bookstores late at night. There, he discovered the books of Evans-Wentz, who drew him specifically to Tibetan Buddhism.

It would be inaccurate to call Gere's first meeting with the Dalai Lama a conversion experience. However, he did come away from that meeting with the strong sense that the teachings of the Dalai Lama were the ones he would follow and the best principles for giving meaning to his life. He describes the Dalai Lama as his "root guru." Gere and the Dalai

Lama have since forged a strong friendship and alliance that has lasted for over 35 years. Gere not only seeks spiritual guidance from the Dalai Lama but has also become a leading spokesperson for the liberation of Tibet from Chinese rule. In 1993, Gere was slated to present at the annual Academy Awards, but he tossed aside the prepared speech he had been assigned by the awards organizers and, instead, delivered an impassioned speech denouncing human rights violations in Tibet and China. Noting that the Academy Awards are broadcast in China, he addressed the Chinese head of state Deng Xiaoping by name, asking him to withdraw from Tibet.

1980s: Attempts at a Chinese Compromise Fail

The 1980s were exciting years for the Dalai Lama. He traveled extensively, taught Buddhist practices to increasingly enthusiastic audiences, continued to lobby for the welfare of Tibet, and rounded out the decade by accepting the Nobel Peace Prize. It was also the decade in which the Dalai Lama pushed hard for improvements in Tibet's relationship with China.

In 1980, Chinese officials began an extended dialogue about Tibet, which led to three official fact-finding visits. Reports on these missions admitted to human rights violations and the low quality of life in Tibet. This report, along with international sympathy for Tibet, induced some much-needed reforms in Chinese-occupied Tibet. Tibetans found themselves, once again, free to speak their own language and practice their religion. Monasteries reopened, albeit with restrictions. The proportion of Tibetan governmental authorities was increased, and some Chinese overlords left.

The Chinese also began to feel that, if they could reconcile with the Dalai Lama, the Tibetan people would be easier to manage. Accordingly, the Chinese government, represented by General Secretary of the Communist Party Hu Yaobang, issued a formal invitation to the Dalai Lama to mend fences with

China. However, their brief, five-point invitation sent mixed messages. It invited the Dalai Lama and his 80,000 exiles to return to Tibet but then recommended that the Dalai Lama not actually live in Tibet or hold office. Instead, it was recommended that he take up residence in Peking, making periodic visits to Tibet.

The Dalai Lama found that he could not respond favorably to this invitation. He and his closest advisors worried that, by accommodating the Chinese, they would forever lose the chance to regain greater autonomy for Tibet. At worst, history might see the Dalai Lama as a traitor to his own cause. So he declined the invitation to return, stating that he could return only if he were satisfied that the Tibetan majority wished to live under Communist rule.

In 1987, the Dalai Lama formally addressed the U.S. Congressional Human Rights Caucus on the issue of Tibet's ongoing occupation by China. There, he introduced a Five Point Peace Plan for Tibet. This plan cited the historic peacefulness of the Tibetan people and states that Tibet had, historically, been an important buffer zone in Asia and its independence had contributed to regional stability. Since

China's invasion, several uprisings had occurred in Tibet and, he noted, tensions were again mounting.

His five-point plan called for making Tibet a "zone of peace," respecting Tibet's human rights and freedoms, restoring Tibet's natural resources, ceasing the production of nuclear weapons and nuclear waste dumping in Tibet, negotiating with China about Tibet's future, and placing a stop order on the relocation of Han Chinese into Tibet. It is worth noting that the Dalai Lama's resistance to Han Chinese immigration was not simple prejudice but rather a recognition that Tibetans were already a minority in Tibet and that the future of Tibetan culture was precarious and unable to withstand further destruction and hybridization.

In 1988, the Dalai Lama issued the Strasbourg Proposal, a formal statement of his middle-way approach to reconciling Tibet's interests with China's. He addressed this statement to the European Parliament. He stated that Tibet was founded in 127 B.C. and, prior the Chinese invasion of 1949, it had never submitted to foreign control. Since that invasion, the Dalai Lama noted, a million Tibet nationals had been killed, monasteries had been destroyed, and children had been deprived of education. He further noted that, because of an aggressive Chinese relocation program that had moved thousands of Han Chinese into Tibet, Tibetans had become a minority in their own country and were treated as second-class citizens. He then reiterated the goals of the Five Point Peace Plan for Tibet that he had unveiled just a year earlier. He stated that he had no ambition to hold a political office in Tibet. He also said that China should understand that forced colonization was anachronistic and impractical in the present day. He claimed that only associations that were made voluntarily, such as the European Parliament and the European Union, were viable. He noted that many Tibetans would be disappointed at a proposal that didn't ask for full autonomy, and he reiterated that he did not wish to see Tibetans resort to violence against China.

The Dalai Lama Sides with Science and Environmentalism

In the late 1980s, a group of Americans founded the Mind and Life Institute as a way of creating a connection between the Dalai Lama and science. Jamphel Yeshe, who had been fascinated by technology and scientific advancements even as a child, welcomed the opportunity to talk about the intersection of science and Buddhist belief. As a result, groups of scientists met with the Dalai Lama at his home in Dharamsala for a series of roundtable discussions.

The Dalai Lama's interest in science led, quite naturally, to a concern for the natural world and the fragility of its resources. In 1986, the Dalai Lama issued a public message in conjunction with World Environment Day. He called for an ethical approach to conserving natural resources, in particular rescuing endangered species. He stated that environmental degradation happens as a consequence of ignorance and greed. In the past, people believed that the rich resources of earth were inexhaustible, but the Dalai Lama asserted that people in the present day, knowing otherwise, were obligated to tap the earth's resources in a sustainable manner.

In the coming decades, he would reiterate this message, advocating at one point for forest conservation in Tibet and at another point demanding a halt to the trade in endangered species products. As he continued to educate himself on scientific issues, his environmental ethos continued to evolve.

In 1989, the Dalai Lama received the Nobel Peace Prize. The Norwegian committee that determines the prize winners applauded the Dalai Lama's consistent opposition to violence in negotiating with China to resolve the problems of Tibet. In explaining their decision, the committee noted that the Dalai Lama had constructed forward-looking solutions to international conflicts.

Committee Chairman Egil Aarvik presented the award, commenting that the Tibetan community in exile is unique because, unlike other such communities, it had not become a militant liberation movement. He also praised the Dalai Lama's conciliatory attitude toward China, which, he noted, was all the more impressive given the terrible sufferings of the Tibetan people. Aarvik compared the Dalai Lama to Mahatma Ghandi.

1990s: The Campaign to Save Tibet's Forests

In the 1990s, the Dalai Lama continued his breakneck schedule of traveling and teaching. But his message became progressively more ecumenical, and true to form, he has frequently offered an opinion on social and political issues over the course of the past three decades. His main message, starting in the 1990s, has been one of global ethics. By "global ethics," the Dalai Lama means that all people must take personal responsibility for ensuring human rights, fairness, equality, and environmental protection, regardless of their belief system. He believes that people need not embrace Buddhism to live good lives. Often he says that practicing Buddhism is unnecessary. Everyone can find the keys to a purposeful and moral life within their own culture and religious framework.

A 1993 *New York Times* interview with the Dalai Lama revealed a man with an ethical system that some might find overly flexible. Others would praise him for his compassion and respect for diversity. In that interview, he expressed a number of views that might have surprised the Buddha and even the most devout monks of early twentieth-century Tibet. He did not shy away from questions about human sexuality and its sometimes unwanted consequences. He expressed deep concern about global overpopulation. The best solution, he indicated, would be to overcome the yearning for sex with mental discipline. When the interviewer pressed him on the subject of birth control, he indicated that the use of birth control does not contradict Buddhist teaching. He also said that, while abortion is a misfortune, it may be the best option if the birth of a child will create a hardship for the parents. Each case should be considered individually, he said.

During the same interview, the Dalai Lama affirmed his belief in the equality of women. Here, he said that Buddhist belief calls unequivocally for women to be respected, though he allowed that women in Tibet had experienced discrimination. He also spoke out against the violent suppression of pro-democracy demonstrations at Tiananmen Square and against the international weapons trade.

In the same year, he formally affirmed these convictions in an address to the United Nations World Conference on Human Rights in Vienna. At that conference, he reiterated his belief that everyone must take responsibility not only for their own family and community but also for the problems of the world, which include overpopulation, environmental degradation, and human rights violations.

The Dalai Lama has expressed a particular concern about environmental impacts and endangered species. In 1996, the Dalai Lama gave a lecture during a trip to Australia. He spoke of the wholesale destruction of forests and animal species in Tibet. Many Tibetans claim that animals in pre-Chinese Tibet were so well-respected that they had little fear of humans. Flocks of birds would roost in the midst of busy human settlements. Flocks of blue sheep and yaks similarly felt no compunction when grazing for food brought them into close association with people. Many Tibetans who have left their country and reported on conditions to the Dalai Lama claim that, when the Chinese first went hunting in Tibet, their gray clothing scared the animals. But when the same hunters donned the traditionally colorful gear of Tibet, the animals showed less fear and became easy targets. These Tibetan exiles further reported, with great sorrow, that entire forests in Tibet had been razed and that many native animals were now sighted only rarely.

The degradation of Tibet's forests, the Dalai Lama noted, has massive impacts on other countries because Tibet is the source of many major rivers that run through Asia. The destruction of forests removes a natural buffer of protection for these rivers, which are in danger of being polluted right at their source.

Reconciling Buddhism and Modern Science

The Dalai Lama has shown an amazing ability to subordinate his Buddhist philosophy to the needs of a changing world. As a consequence, his message has become more and more current even as he pushes on the back door of eighty years. One of his most remarkable reforms is to state unequivocally that religion should not oppose itself to science. "Where Buddhist teachings contradict science, science should prevail," he has said.

In 2003, the Dalai Lama accepted an invitation to attend a symposium at the Massachusetts Institute of Technology, titled "Investigating the Mind." Jamphel Yeshe was, at the time, on a three-week tour of the United States, but he described the MIT symposium as the most important stop on that trip. The symposium brought together a group of Buddhist monks and a hand-picked panel of specialists in the fields of cognitive science and neuroscience. MIT's Kresge auditorium was able to hold fewer than half the people who had jockeyed for invitations to the event. The 1,200 lucky audience members were a mix of Buddhists, scientists and other academics, journalists, and two A-list film stars—Richard Gere and Goldie Hawn. Organized and financed by the Mind and Life Institute, the goal of the symposium was to revisit the apparent contradiction between science and Buddhist tradition.

The Tibetan spiritual leader showed up at MIT fresh from a meeting with former United States president George W. Bush. In the discussions that ensued, the Dalai Lama frequently found parallels between the findings of cognitive science and Buddhist teachings. During introductory comments that kick-started the event, Adam Engle—the Institute's chairman—said that science had been wrong in rejecting out of hand the Buddhist model for investigating the human mind.

The "Investigating the Mind" symposium paved the way for a long-standing relationship between the Dalai Lama and MIT. In 2009, following another invitation to speak at MIT, he gave a lecture on ethics. His message was that educators must find a way to teach compassion and moral values apart from a religious context. That statement was the framework for what became the Dalai Lama Center for Ethics and Transformative Values at MIT. The Dalai Lama is a frequent guest and speaker at the Center.

The Dalai Lama's affirmation of science is linked to his advocacy for natural resources. In 2005, he liaised with two environmental organizations—the Wildlife Trust of India and Care for the Wild International—in calling for the protection of Tibet's forests. In 2006, the Dalai Lama was outraged to learn from environmentalists that the importation of tiger skins into Tibet was a major contributor to the extinction of tigers in Asia. And this time, it was not the Chinese who were to blame: tiger skins were being used in making chubas, the traditional coat that Tibetans wear. Historically, these coats were made of sheepskin. It is unclear at what point Tibetans started using tiger skins in their garments, but the skins were being brazenly traded in Tibetan markets long after such trading had been made illegal by international laws. In a public address, the Dalai Lama scolded the thousands of Tibetan pilgrims who had traveled to India to celebrate Kalachakra, a Buddhist holy day. He was ashamed that his people would participate in the decimation of a wild animal species.

What happened next was an amazing testament to the ongoing power that the Dalai Lama exercises in Tibet. The travelers returned to Tibet, and many of them immediately burned their tiger skins, even though they were worth approximately two years' wages apiece. By this act, they honored the Dalai Lama's edict to end the exploitation of

Asia's tigers. The word of the exiled Dalai Lama spread throughout Tibet, and soon the skies were filled with the smoke and smell of burning tiger skin. In 2013, the *Economist* reported that the Dalai Lama's proclamation had single-handedly put an end to Tibet's trade in tiger skins. Today, Tibet is a safe haven for snow leopards and other large cats, which enjoy protection programs enforced by the monks.

The Dalai Lama continued his campaign for the protection of Tibet's forests in 2010, when he gave interviews to several news agencies in which he decried China's failure to protect Tibet's natural assets. The Dalai Lama noted the link between deforestation and extreme weather events in China and elsewhere in Asia. The Chinese, he admitted, had imposed some regulations on cutting, but due to governmental corruption, it was far too easy to flout these rules. Businessmen had only to offer a bribe to get around tree ordinances.

In 2010, the Dalai Lama broadened his environmental message to include a concern about worldwide climate change. On the Tibetan plateau, temperatures were rising at more than twice the average global rate, a phenomenon that could have devastating implications, not just for Tibet but for the rest of Asia and beyond, if the Himalayan icebergs should melt. During a ten-day tour of Australia, he urged world leaders to put the interests of the planet above their countries' short-term interests. He described climate change as the first and most pressing issue the world faces.

The Dalai Lama's many achievements in the first decade of the twenty-first century were somewhat overshadowed by protests that erupted concerning his repudiation of the god Dorje Shugden decades earlier. In Oxford, England, a thousand Buddhists turned out to protest the Dalai Lama's 2008 visit. They were members of the Western Shugden Society, a Buddhist sect that still honors Shugden in defiance of the Dalai Lama's edict. Signs accused the Tibetan leader of lying, and protesters told the local media that the Dalai Lama supported human rights abuses against practitioners of Shugden Buddhism. Many of the same protesters followed the Dalai Lama to Nottingham and London, where they enacted further protests. The protesters claimed that the Dalai Lama had prohibited a prayer that is central to the practice of Shugdenism.

It is worth noting that the Dalai Lama never placed a ban on learning or teaching the principles of Shugdenism. His concern was that Shugdenism was a divisive and fundamentalist movement within Buddhism that would hurt its global solidarity.

This controversy also has a great deal to do with conflicting beliefs about Dorje Shugden. One thread of Buddhist belief sees the god as a wise protector while another thread believes that he is a malevolent force akin to a demon. The Dalai Lama, who holds the latter belief, sees the practice of Shugdenism as a type of demon worship, so opposing it is, for him, a matter of common sense.

The surge of anger against the Dalai Lama, over 30 years after his denunciation of the *Yellow Book*, corresponds to an unexpected growth of Shugden Buddhism in Western countries. Meindert Gorter, a Dutch Buddhist and Shugden practitioner, published a series of blogs in the *New Statesman* explaining that there was no need to blend the various Buddhist traditions and that doing so was like mixing a banana split with apple pie.

It is safe to say that the Dalai Lama's reservations about Shugdenism are largely based in his increasingly ecumenical religious outlook. Where Dorje Shugden followers wish to observe a narrowly-defined religious tradition that excludes all other traditions, the Dalai Lama seeks to find common ground not only between the various denominations of Buddhism but between all the major world religions.

That was the impulse that drove him to inaugurate the World Religions Dialogue and Symphony in 2009. Located in the small coastal town of Mahuva in India's Bhavnagar district, the event spanned six days. Religious leaders of all faiths and from all over the world convened for lectures and discussions. The Dalai Lama explained that the purpose of the event was to achieve peace through discussion. He added that it was important for such conversations to occur even if they do not produce immediate results.

Stalled Negotiations with China

During the first decade of the twentieth century, the Dalai Lama met with Chinese leaders in a series of meetings aimed at coming to terms with the question of Tibet's autonomy. The result of these meetings was invariably the same. The Chinese demanded the dissolution of the Tibet government-in-exile, and they also demanded that the Dalai Lama cease traveling and representing Tibet. The Dalai Lama continued to lobby for a Tibet with real religious and cultural freedom and an autonomous local government.

The year 2008 brought new urgency to these negotiations. In that year, Tibetans once again rose up violently against Chinese rule. It was the worst conflict since the Lhasa uprising in 1959. The conflict erupted just before the Beijing Olympics, and the Chinese saw the protests as an attempt to hurt the nation's reputation and tarnish the prestige of playing host to the international games. The timing of this uprising, however, may have had more to do with the 1959 Lhasa uprising, which took place exactly 49 years earlier. The monks and nuns who were the chief participants in the uprising were more likely to be sensitive to the anniversary of their spiritual leader's exodus from Tibet than to the far-off games in Beijing.

The uprising started with 500 monks attempting to march on Lhasa and being stopped, beaten, and arrested as a result. The conflict escalated from there, with other monks holding street protests to denounce the imprisonment of their colleagues. Rumors flew that the captive monks were being starved and beaten and that some had even been murdered.

World leaders, including President George W. Bush of the United States, called on China to meet with the Dalai Lama again and attempt a compromise. China was never in greater need of a peaceful solution to Tibet's anger about ongoing Chinese occupation. Despite that, the talks between Chinese leaders and the Dalai Lama broke down. It didn't help that the Chinese loudly blamed the Dalai Lama for the riots, calling his followers a "clique." Tibetans, however, have denied that the Dalai Lama was in any way involved with the uprising. Some of them have noted that the uprising would have been much worse had the Dalai Lama backed it.

It was under these strained circumstances that the Dalai Lama met with Chinese authorities in the southern Chinese town of Shenzhen. According to staff reports, the Dalai Lama asked for Tibetan prisoners to be released and for the Chinese to desist from requiring monks to repudiate the Dalai Lama formally.

The Chinese were not forthcoming and issued no statements concerning their part in the talks. As the talks were taking place, China's President Hu Jintao said that he was hopeful that such resumed communication would bring about a satisfactory result. However, his message was badly undermined by the government-owned media, which continued to blame the Dalai Lama for trying to divide China and trying to ruin the Chinese Olympics. The talks broke down, having made no progress. The Dalai Lama met with the Chinese again in 2010. Talks again broke down with no progress made. As of this writing, that was the Dalai Lama's last attempt to negotiate in person with the Chinese, who routinely refer to Tibet's spiritual leader as a "wolf in monk's clothing."

The Chinese view of the Dalai Lama is very different from the mental picture of him held by the rest of the world. Worldwide, the Dalai Lama is recognized as a leading advocate of peace and individual spiritual development. The Chinese media, however, portrays a man who took advantage of his feudal privilege, who resisted the peaceful "liberation" of Tibet by the Chinese, and who incites violence by innuendo. When the Dalai Lama indicates that his non-violent approach to Tibet's occupation may not be honored after his death, the

Chinese media construes it as a call to arms. Even Chinese nationals who live overseas see the respect afforded to the Dalai Lama as an affront to China's reputation and solidarity.

Chinese authorities may sincerely believe that, if it were not for the Dalai Lama, ethnic Tibetans would by now have settled happily into the role of law-abiding Communists. It is more certain that the Dalai Lama has become a magnet for the Chinese dismay that Tibet still hates being part of China. The Dalai Lama's repeated failure over several decades to negotiate a peaceful co-existence between Tibet and China may be one reason that he has now resigned as secular leader of the exiled Tibet community.

Travel Alternates with Solitude

In recent years, the Dalai Lama's life has followed a strict schedule. He reserves five months of the year for solitude and meditation in his home in Dharamsala. There, he rises at 3:30 or 4:00 in the morning. His yellow brick house is unostentatious, but it does feature banks of tall windows that provide light and views in many directions. Statues and paintings of Buddha are the principal decor items, along with a relief map on which the mountains of Tibet rise higher than any other part of the world.

He places a thin, narrow prayer cushion on the floor and lowers himself on to it several times, demonstrating amazing agility for a man of his age. He may take a minute to gaze out at the mountains from his balcony. He may spend a few minutes running on a treadmill. Outside, monkeys scream, and an armed guard, dressed in beige combat fatigues, keeps vigil. During his period of solitude, the Dalai Lama meditates, reads, and writes. He has written and published over a dozen books and co-authored others. As the day passes, he frequently finds something worthy of a chuckle—a soft, almost completely silent laugh. In the evenings, he watches television, taking particular care to keep up with events in China.

During the seven months he is not in seclusion, he is almost never alone, except in the early morning. Every minute is budgeted. When he is not on the road, droves of tourists, spiritual seekers, and Buddhist monks and nuns make their way to see him. There is not enough room in his private temple for everyone who desires an audience.

The Dalai Lama teaches that the self lies somewhere beyond our bodies and our minds. He preaches that human nature is essentially good. Only the affection of a mother allows a child to survive. Only the baby's affection for his mother drives him to feed from her breast. This shows, the Dalai Lama explains, that we are born into compassion and sustained by it. So our essential nature is compassionate.

But these days, he does a lot more than simply dispense Buddhist philosophy. He also deplores the sharp distinctions between rich and poor that exist in many countries. He notes that the world's population has accelerated wildly since 1950. At present, the earth may have enough resources to sustain the six billion people there are now, but it does not have enough to sustain another doubling of the population. The solution, he says with a smile, is to have more monks and nuns. The other solution, he adds more practically, is to use birth control.

Outside his temple are Buddhist prayer wheels—large, rotating metal cylinders engraved with a multitude of prayers. As they depart the temple, many of the pilgrims roll these wheels, sending prayers out into the wider world.

Resignation of Secular Authority

On March 10, 2011, the Dalai Lama addressed a packed audience at the Buddhist temple in Dharamsala. March 10 marks the anniversary of the Lhasa uprising against the Chinese, and the Dalai Lama honors the memory of that event every year by giving a talk to local Tibetans in exile. But this year, the exiles were shocked to hear the Dalai Lama announce his resignation from secular authority. Though the Central Tibetan Authority had been established in the 1960s to offer a democratic form of government to the exiles, the Dalai Lama had still been its de facto head of state. However, in 2011, he decided to withdraw from that position and demanded that Tibetans in exile vote to elect a new leader. In the same speech, he called for an amendment to the Charter for Tibetans in Exile that would formally remove him from the political sphere. That charter amendment, which was subsequently approved, gave greater power to the elected prime minister of the Tibetan government-in-exile.

The Dalai Lama said that he would remain, as always, a spiritual guide and teacher and that he would continue to support the people of Tibet. But, he joked, he did not want to end up like the queen, reading bad speeches written by someone else. This announcement elicited strong feelings from the Tibetan exiles, many of whom begged the Dalai Lama to remain at his political post or, at least, to retain some symbolic political position. Samdhong Rinpoche, the Central Tibetan Authority's prime minister at that time, said that the Dalai Lama's resignation could destabilize the exile community, which had cohered so long largely out of love and respect for the Dalai Lama.

The Dalai Lama was firm in his decision, however. He had long been a believer in the separation of church and state. It would be hypocritical to continue as both a secular and religious leader, he explained. And he just wanted to be a simple monk. Monarchy was a thing of the past and theocracy a thing of the far past, the Dalai Lama explained, adding that the future lay with democracy. His retirement from politics was a bold break with tradition. Most of the fourteen Dalai Lamas have wielded power both as spiritual leader and as king. However, Jamphel Yeshe could call upon the precedent of the first Dalai Lama, Gendun Drup, who was a monk and highly respected teacher but who never held a political office.

In an interview with the German newspaper *Der Spiegel*, the Dalai Lama revealed that he had a further agenda in stepping down. The Chinese had loudly insisted that the Dalai Lama was the chief obstacle in successful negotiations with Tibet.

Now, China would not have that excuse. By renouncing political power, the Dalai Lama felt he could force China to negotiate a lasting peace with Tibet or lay its true cards on the table for the world to see.

The Dalai Lama's retirement from government may also have been intended to make it easier for him to meet with world leaders. The Dalai Lama has frequently met with the most powerful leaders of the world, including United States Presidents Ronald Reagan, Bill Clinton, George W. Bush, and Barack Obama. But such meetings always occupy a grey area. China still characterized meetings with the Dalai Lama as interference with China's domestic affairs. So such meetings, though highly publicized, were informal and unofficial.

Another good reason for the Dalai Lama to resign was that some people openly accused him of harboring plans to retake Tibet and re-impose the pre-communist feudal system. Though this ambition seems highly unlikely to anyone who has seriously researched the Dalai Lama's career, it is true that Tibet was governed on feudal principles prior to the Chinese invasion. Under this system, peasants were tied to land that was not in their ownership and could be brutally punished for insubordination to their feudal lords who were the landowners. Jamphel Yeshe's predecessor, the thirteenth Dalai Lama, had begun reforms, but they had not gone far enough, and the fourteenth Dalai Lama was still a child when the Chinese invaded his country and pre-empted his authority. Jamphel Yeshe is on record as admitting that Tibet's feudal system lent itself to abuses and needed reform. And he has, for many years, expressed his admiration for the democratic government in India. His resignation from government demonstrates, conclusively, that he has no ambition to be a feudal king.

The Dalai Lama emphasized that his resignation from the secular realm had nothing to do with health. Several reports from this period corroborate that, at 76, the Dalai Lama was quite healthy. Certainly, his grueling travel and lecture schedule would be impossible for a man who was not in peak physical condition.

The following August, Lobsang Sangay was democratically elected and installed as the new prime minister of Tibet in exile, a population that was reported to be 100,000 strong in that year. Contrary to its promise, China immediately reversed its position on the Dalai Lama. Chinese leaders refused to meet with Sangay and have declared they will now only negotiate with an envoy of the Dalai Lama. Sangay noted that Tibet's exiles resisted the Dalai Lama's resignation, but he also observed that these were the same people who told the Dalai Lama in the 1960s that they did not need a parliament because they had a Dalai Lama.

The Dalai Lama's retirement from politics dovetailed with the announcement of a new law in China regarding the Dalai Lama. Chinese authorities declared that, by law, the Dalai Lama must reincarnate in China and his legitimacy must be recognized by the Chinese government. Chinese law has, for many years, dictated that the appointment of high lamas must receive the government's stamp of approval, one of many policies that incite resentment in Tibet. It is clear to most political analysts that China means to make the next Dalai Lama a Chinese propagandist. Many people have speculated that in the future there could be two Dalai Lamas, one appointed by the Chinese and one discovered by the Tibetan lamas, who do not recognize China's right to rule in Tibet, much less its right to name a Dalai Lama.

The Chinese have already demonstrated their willingness to force their choices on the monastic community by their appointment of the Panchen Lama. The Panchen Lama is the second-highest-ranking monk in Tibetan Buddhist tradition. Like the Dalai Lama, he controls the circumstances of his next incarnation. The Dalai Lama named Gedhun Choekyi Nyima, a young Tibetan, as the eleventh Panchen Lama on May 14, 1995. Only three days later, the Chinese put the child under house arrest, and he has not been seen since. The Chinese replaced Gedhun Choekyi Nyima with their own choice for Panchen Lama—Gyaincain Norbu. Gyaincain Norbu was born in Tibet to two loyal members of the Chinese communist party. After his appointment to the post of Panchen Lama, he was whisked away to China to be educated in Beijing under the influence of unadulterated communism. When he returned to Tibet as a young adult, he was stricken with altitude sickness because he was unaccustomed to life in the high mountains.

Exiled Tibetans do not acknowledge Gyaincain Norbu as the true Panchen Lama, nor do the Chinese acknowledge the successor identified by the Dalai Lama. The existence of an official and unofficial Panchen Lama suggests the possibility of two future Dalai Lamas in conflict.

So it is not terribly surprising that the buzz surrounding the Dalai Lama's resignation from government morphed almost seamlessly into speculations about his next incarnation. A journalist at the *Guardian*, one of London's leading newspapers, conjectured that the Dalai Lama's resignation from the political sphere would open the door for him to name his successor during his lifetime, thus pre-empting any attempt by the Chinese to make a puppet of the next Dalai Lama.

But that's not what happened. Instead, in 2011, the Dalai Lama made the shocking announcement that he might choose not to reincarnate at all. He told the media that, when he was 90, he would consult with Buddhist leaders about whether the position of the Dalai Lama should continue or whether it has served its purpose and run its course. He also said that, should he choose to continue his earthly existence, he would leave written instructions to guide the discovery of the fifteenth Dalai Lama. The purpose of any Dalai Lama is to complete the task of the former, he explained. And because he lives outside Tibet, the fifteenth Dalai Lama will definitely be born outside Tibet if the institution continues. The Dalai Lama has also suggested that the fifteenth Dalai Lama could be female.

Worldwide, journalists and political commentators are in agreement that, by this move, the Dalai Lama means to stop the Chinese from making the next Dalai Lama a puppet of the government. From a Buddhist point of view, the idea that the Chinese can "appoint" their own Dalai Lama is a nonsensical notion. According to Buddhism, no human or human organization can dictate or control another human's reincarnation. Most people are reborn in a higher or lower position based on how they led their lives (i.e., their karma). Someone whose life was mostly motivated by greed, who allowed his or her karma to rot, may be reincarnated as a yak or even an insect. Someone who devoted his or her life to virtue may be reincarnated as a human occupying a position of greater privilege. Only a few Buddhists can control the terms of their reincarnation. These are the Bodhisattvas, who return to human form out of compassion for others because they wish to serve the human race. As a Bodhisattva, the Dalai Lama has always chosen the circumstances of his rebirth, as do other high-ranking lamas such as the Panchen Lama. Only a country of entrenched atheists could be so cynical as to propose that they could dictate the reincarnation of a sincere Buddhist.

It is a tradition for the Dalai Lama to express some reservations about reincarnating; in the Buddhist tradition, such reluctance is an important gesture of humility. But many analysts believe that, in keeping his reincarnation options open, the Dalai Lama is playing one of his last chips in a decades-long game with the Chinese. He is, perhaps, signaling to the Chinese that their last chance to negotiate with the Dalai Lama will die with him. Some people think it's the Dalai Lama's last-ditch effort to be readmitted to Tibet. If the last Dalai Lama dies in exile, more than one generation of Tibetan will never get to see their esteemed spiritual leader even once. It is a crime against their culture that they may never forgive.

China Strikes Back

After roughly 47 years on the road, teaching Buddhist principles and creating awareness for Tibet, the Dalai Lama has of late found himself less welcome in foreign lands than he had previously. China has labeled the Dalai Lama a separatist whose goal of a freer Tibet makes him a state enemy. Meanwhile, China has become a formidable presence in international trade. That has led some nations to deny visas or refuse talks with the Dalai Lama simply because they feel they cannot afford to alienate China.

United States President Barack Obama has met with the Dalai Lama three times, defying Chinese anger. Prior to their most recent meeting, in February of 2014, Hua Chunying, a Chinese Foreign Ministry Spokeswoman said that, in meeting with the Dalai Lama, the United States was "grossly" interfering with China's sovereign policy and damaging relations between the United States and China. Like the majority of United States presidents before him, however, Obama has been openly sympathetic to the plight of Tibet, and he supports the preservation of Tibet's historic culture, religion, and language. Obama endorses the Dalai Lama's middle way, which seeks better freedoms for Tibet but not necessarily a break with China. The two leaders met in the map room of the White House, and no reporters were allowed to attend. In a separate statement after his meeting with the Dalai Lama, Obama reiterated that he does not seek independence for Tibet.

But other nations have buckled under Chinese pressure not to receive the Dalai Lama. Many Norwegians were shocked to learn that Norway's leaders refused an invitation to parlay with the Dalai Lama when he visited Norway in May 2014. Norway's Prime Minister Erna Solberg made a public statement that the country's decision not to meet with the Dalai Lama was motivated by a desire to improve communication and diplomatic relations with China. Though the Dalai Lama was warmly welcomed to Norway by over a thousand fans, who gathered outside the Grand Hotel to see him, it was alarming that the country that had selected him for the highest international peace prize 25 years earlier now considered him a slightly toxic asset. That assessment was by no means universal, however. The Nobel Norwegian Committee, having issued the invitation in the first place, was happy to receive the Dalai Lama. Additionally, many Norwegians questioned the Prime Minister's decision, feeling that the cost of China's goodwill was too high.

A few months later, South Africa refused to grant the Dalai Lama a visitor's visa. He had applied for access to South Africa in order to attend the Fourteenth World Summit of Nobel Peace Laureates. It was the third time in five years that the Dalai Lama's application for a visa had been denied. As in Norway, the government's decision was swathed in controversy and protests. Four women, all former Nobel Peace Prize winners, boycotted the summit in protest against the Dalai Lama's exclusion. Jody Williams, an American activist; Shirin Ebadi, an Iranian attorney and activist; and Leymah Gbowee, a Liberian anti-landmine activist, issued a statement that China was inappropriately pressuring other countries to restrict the Dalai Lama's travel because of his historical connection to an independent Tibet. In addition, fourteen former prize-winners signed a letter to President Jacob Zuma of South Africa, requesting that the Dalai Lama be admitted to South Africa and predicting damage to South Africa's international reputation if another refusal were made. The Dalai Lama himself accused the South African government of "bullying" him. Denial of the Dalai Lama's visa led directly to the cancellation of the summit, with organizers expressing regret and saying it would be held at some other time—someplace other than South Africa.

Late in 2014, the Dalai Lama informally requested China to allow him to visit Tibet and China. Specifically, he wished to make a holy pilgrimage to Mount Wutai in China's Shanxi province. Mount Wutai is particularly sacred to Chinese Buddhists and is the home of over twenty temples that lie on or near the mountain. Predictably, the Chinese denied the Dalai Lama's request. Hong Lei, a spokesperson for China's foreign ministry, said in effect that the Dalai Lama does not need to return to Tibet. He needs, instead, to quit trying to split China.

But politicians represent a small fraction of the world's population, and enthusiasm for the Dalai Lama has grown to such an extent that competition to attend one of his lectures is fierce. Gone are the days of half-empty lecture halls that greeted the Dalai Lama on his first tour of the United States. In 2014, Princeton University announced that the Dalai Lama would be part of its speaker series. Jadwin Gymnasium, where the event took place, seated 4,000 people. Most of the available seats were reserved for the university's faculty, staff, and students, but 1,000 tickets were made available to the general public via the internet. When they went up for sale, they were all purchased within three minutes.

The Dalai Lama's "Develop the Heart" lecture at Princeton was typical of the lectures he gives to college students. At these events, he emphasizes the importance of developing compassion while developing intellect. Many universities have recorded the Dalai Lama's lectures and made them available on the internet, which allows the world to glimpse the Dalai Lama in action. At the University of Oregon, the Dalai Lama took the stage wearing his traditional red monk's robe, trimmed with yellow and purple. It is a modest garment that falls to his ankles while leaving his rake-thin left arm exposed. To this, he added a green University of Oregon visor with the letter "O" in the front, which cast a shadow over his forehead and his timeless, wire-rimmed glasses. He addressed his audience as "my brothers and sisters," as he always does. His English was rusty and frequently unidiomatic, but he was a skillful orator nonetheless, making excellent use of dramatic pauses and minimalistic hand gestures. He noted that we are all humans who share a common emotional concern: we all want to be happy. But our happiness depends on the actions of the rest of the world, so it behooves us to develop global perspective. Many of our problems—poverty, bullying, and violence—are man-made problems that are within our control. These problems emerge because we forget the oneness of humanity. We need to look past the secondary level of differences and make sacrifices, he explained.

Conclusion

What does the Dalai Lama's life teach us? Certainly, he is a sterling example of turning adversity into joyful service. But there is more to him than that: he is also a model of innovation and adaptation. He has taken the tenets of Buddhism and made them relevant to everyone. His message is not just about personal happiness and good karma; it is also very much about respecting the earth's resources, recognizing the equality of all people, and sharing with the less fortunate. He has said that, at 90 years, he will decide whether his long series of lives as the Dalai Lama will end. As of this writing, he is nearly 80 years old. Will he live another ten years? We can only hope so. As weapons of destruction grow ever more sophisticated and populations continue to polarize, the world desperately needs to hear his lessons on cooperation and non-violence.

In October 2014, the Dalai Lama accepted a long-life prayer from Keutsang Rinpoche. According to Buddhist belief, this is the same man who identified the fourteenth Dalai Lama as a two-year-old boy in Taktser. He died and was reborn in Communist-run Tibet in 1944. He languished in a Chinese prison for eighteen years because he dared to bless the Tibetan rebels who participated in the Lhasa uprising of 1959. In 1985, he made his way, weak and starved, to Dharamsala.

There, like so many other Tibetan refugees before him, he was warmly welcomed by the Dalai Lama, who helped him rebuild his life in India. The long-life prayer ceremony took place in Dharamsala's main temple. Speaking to the media about the ceremony, Keutsang Rinpoche said that there was not much he could do in return for the help he has received from the Dalai Lama, but he could offer this prayer.

The long life-prayer for the Dalai Lama called on the deities of three worlds and asked them to bestow on Jamphel Yeshe a life of 100 eons and the time to fulfill his purpose. That's a sentiment that echoes in the minds of people all over the world.

Please enjoy the first two chapters of Pope Francis: Pastor of Mercy, written by Michael J. Ruszala, as available from Wyatt North Publishing.

Pope Francis: Pastor of Mercy
Chapter 1

There is something about Pope Francis that captivates and delights people, even people who hardly know anything about him. He was elected in only two days of the conclave, yet many who tried their hand at speculating on who the next pope might be barely included him on their lists. The evening of Wednesday, March 13, 2013, the traditional white smoke poured out from the chimney of the Sistine Chapel and spread throughout the world by way of television, Internet, radio, and social media, signaling the beginning of a new papacy.

As the light of day waned from the Eternal City, some 150,000 people gathered watching intently for any movement behind the curtained door to the loggia of St. Peter's. A little after 8:00 p.m., the doors swung open and Cardinal Tauran emerged to pronounce the traditional and joyous Latin formula to introduce the new Bishop of Rome: "Annuncio vobis gaudium magnum; habemus papam!" ("I announce to you a great joy: we have a pope!") He then announced the new Holy Father's identity: "Cardinalem Bergoglio..."

The name Bergoglio, stirred up confusion among most of the faithful who flooded the square that were even more clueless than the television announcers were, who scrambled to figure out who exactly the new pope was. Pausing briefly, Cardinal

Tauran continued by announcing the name of the new pope: "...qui sibi nomen imposuit Franciscum" ("who takes for himself the name Francis"). Whoever this man may be, his name choice resonated with all, and the crowd erupted with jubilant cheers. A few moments passed before the television announcers and their support teams informed their global audiences that the man who was about to walk onto the loggia dressed in white was Cardinal Jorge Mario Bergoglio, age 76, of Buenos Aires, Argentina.

To add to the bewilderment and kindling curiosity, when the new pope stepped out to the thunderous applause of the crowd in St. Peter's Square, he did not give the expected papal gesture of outstretched arms. Instead, he gave only a simple and modest wave. Also, before giving his first apostolic blessing, he bowed asking the faithful, from the least to the greatest, to silently pray for him. These acts were only the beginning of many more words and gestures, such as taking a seat on the bus with the cardinals, refusing a popemobile with bulletproof glass, and paying his own hotel bill after his election, that would raise eyebrows among some familiar with papal customs and delight the masses.

Is he making a pointed critique of previous pontificates? Is he simply posturing a persona to the world at large to make a point? The study of the life of Jorge Mario Bergoglio gives a clear answer, and the answer is no. This is simply who he is as a man and as a priest. The example of his thought- provoking gestures flows from his character, his life experiences, his religious vocation, and his spirituality. This book uncovers the life of the 266th Bishop of Rome, Jorge Mario Bergoglio, also known as Father Jorge, a name he preferred even while he was an archbishop and cardinal.

What exactly do people find so attractive about Pope Francis? Aldo Cagnoli, a layman who developed a friendship with the Pope when he was serving as a cardinal, shares the following: "The greatness of the man, in my humble opinion lies not in building walls or seeking refuge behind his wisdom and office, but rather in dealing with everyone judiciously, respectfully, and with humility, being willing to learn at any moment of life; that is what Father Bergoglio means to me" (as quoted in Ch. 12 of Pope Francis: Conversations with Jorge Bergoglio, previously published as El Jesuita [The Jesuit]).

At World Youth Day 2013, in Rio de Janeiro, Brazil, three million young people came out to celebrate their faith with

Pope Francis. Doug Barry, from EWTN's Life on the Rock, interviewed youth at the event on what features stood out to them about Pope Francis. The young people seemed most touched by his authenticity. One young woman from St. Louis said, "He really knows his audience. He doesn't just say things to say things... And he is really sincere and genuine in all that he does." A friend agreed: "He was looking out into the crowd and it felt like he was looking at each one of us...." A young man from Canada weighed in: "You can actually relate to [him]... for example, last night he was talking about the World Cup and athletes." A young woman added, "I feel he means what he says... he practices what he preaches... he states that he's there for the poor and he actually means it."

The Holy Spirit guided the College of Cardinals in its election of Pope Francis to meet the needs of the Church following the historic resignation of Pope Benedict XVI due to old age. Representing the growth and demographic shift in the Church throughout the world and especially in the Southern Hemisphere, Pope Francis is the first non-European pope in almost 1,300 years. He is also the first Jesuit pope. Pope Francis comes with a different background and set of experiences. Both as archbishop and as pope, his flock knows him for his humility, ascetic frugality in solidarity with the poor, and closeness. He was born in Buenos Aires to a family of Italian immigrants, earned a diploma in chemistry, and followed a priestly vocation in the Jesuit order after an experience of God's mercy while receiving the sacrament of Reconciliation. Even though he is known for his smile and humor, the world also recognizes Pope Francis as a stern figure that stands against the evils of the world and challenges powerful government officials, when necessary.

The Church he leads is one that has been burdened in the West by the aftermath of sex abuse scandals and increased secularism. It is also a Church that is experiencing shifting in numbers out of the West and is being challenged with religious persecution in the Middle East, Asia, and Africa. The Vatican that Pope Francis has inherited is plagued by cronyism and scandal. This Holy Father knows, however, that his job is not merely about numbers, politics, or even success. He steers clear of pessimism knowing that he is the head of Christ's Body on earth and works with Christ's grace. This is the man God has chosen in these times to lead his flock.

Chapter 2: Early Life in Argentina

Jorge Mario Bergoglio was born on December 17, 1936, in the Flores district of Buenos Aires. The district was a countryside locale outside the main city during the nineteenth century and many rich people in its early days called this place home. By the time Jorge was born, Flores was incorporated into the city of Buenos Aires and became a middle class neighborhood. Flores is also the home of the beautiful Romantic-styled Basilica of San José de Flores, built in 1831, with its dome over the altar, spire over the entrance, and columns at its facade. It was the Bergoglios' parish church and had much significance in Jorge's life.

Jorge's father's family had arrived in Argentina in 1929, immigrating from Piedimonte in northern Italy. They were not the only ones immigrating to the country. In the late nineteenth century, Argentina became industrialized and the government promoted immigration from Europe. During that time, the land prospered and Buenos Aires earned the moniker "Paris of the South." In the late nineteenth and early twentieth centuries waves of immigrants from Italy, Spain, and other European countries came off ships in the port of Buenos Aires. Three of Jorge's great uncles were the first in the family to immigrate to Argentina in 1922 searching for better employment opportunities after World War I. They established a paving company in Buenos Aires and built a four-story building for their company with the city's first elevator. Jorge's father and paternal grandparents followed the brothers in order to keep the family together and to escape Mussolini's fascist regime in Italy. Jorge's father and grandfather also helped with the business for a time. His father, Mario, who had been an accountant for a rail company in Italy, provided similar services for the family business (Cardinal Bergoglio recalls more on the story of his family's immigration and his early life in Ch. 1 of Conversations with Jorge Bergoglio).

Providentially, the Bergoglios were long delayed in liquidating their assets in Italy; this forced them to miss the ship they planned to sail on, the doomed Pricipessa Mafalda, which sank off the northern coast of Brazil before reaching Buenos Aires. The family took the Giulio Cesare instead and arrived safely in Argentina with Jorge's Grandma Rosa. Grandma Rosa wore a fur coat stuffed with the money the family brought with them from Italy. Economic hard times eventually hit Argentina in 1932 and the family's paving business went under, but the Bergoglio brothers began anew.

Jorge's father, Mario, met his mother Regina at Mass in 1934. Regina was born in Argentina, but her parents were also Italian immigrants. Mario and Regina married the following year after meeting. Jorge, the eldest of their five children, was born in 1936. Jorge fondly recalls his mother gathering the children around the radio on Sunday afternoons to listen to opera and explain the story. A true porteño, as the inhabitants of the port city of Buenos Aires are called, Jorge liked to play soccer, listen to Latin music, and dance the tango. Jorge's paternal grandparents lived around the corner from his home. He greatly admired his Grandma Rosa, and keeps her written prayer for her grandchildren with him until this day. Jorge recalls that while his grandparents kept their personal conversations in Piedmontese, Mario chose mostly to speak Spanish, preferring to look forward rather than back. Still, Jorge grew up speaking both Italian and Spanish.

Upon entering secondary school at the age of thirteen, his father insisted that Jorge begin work even though the family, in their modest lifestyle, was not particularly in need of extra income. Mario Bergoglio wanted to teach the boy the value of work and found several jobs for him during his adolescent years. Jorge worked in a hosiery factory for several years as a cleaner and at a desk. When he entered technical school to study food chemistry, Jorge found a job working in a laboratory. He worked under a woman who always challenged him to do his work thoroughly. He remembers her, though, with both fondness and sorrow. Years later, she was kidnapped and murdered along with members of her family because of her political views during the Dirty War, a conflict in the 1970's and 80's between the military dictatorship and guerrilla fighters in which thousands of Argentineans disappeared.

Initially unhappy with his father's decision to make him work, Jorge recalls later in his life that work was a valuable formative experience for him that taught him responsibility, realism, and how the world operated. He learned that a person's self worth often comes from their work, which led him to become committed later in life to promote a just culture of work rather than simply encouraging charity or entitlement. He believes that people need meaningful work in order to thrive. During his boyhood through his priestly ministry, he experienced the gulf in Argentina between the poor and the well off, which left the poor having few opportunities for gainful employment.

At the age of twenty-one, Jorge became dangerously ill. He was diagnosed with severe pneumonia and cysts. Part of his upper right lung was removed, and each day Jorge endured the pain and discomfort of saline fluid pumped through his chest to clear his system. Jorge remembers that the only person that was able to comfort him during this time was a religious sister who had catechized him from childhood, Sister Dolores. She exposed him to the true meaning of suffering with this simple statement: "You are imitating Christ." This stuck with him, and his sufferings during that time served as a crucible for his character, teaching him how to distinguish what is important in life from what is not. He was being prepared for what God was calling him to do in life, his vocation.

Made in the USA
Las Vegas, NV
02 January 2023

64806999R00079